Thirty Years In September

A NURSE'S MEMOIR

KATE GENOVESE

PUBLISHSED BY FIDELI PUBLISHING INC.

Copyright 2013, Kate Genovese

All rights reserved.

No part of this book may be reproduced or shared by any electronic or mechanical means, including but not limited to printing, file sharing, and email, without prior written permission from Fideli Publishing.

ISBN: 978-1-60414-668-4

PROLOGUE

April 1968

The white walls were sterile looking, the floors shiny, clean, even glistening as I entered into Canton Children's Hospital. The smell of antiseptic was exuding into my olfactory senses.

There was an overweight nurse in a starched uniform, white nylons and a blue sweater. A white cap stood firmly on her head; I was frightened of her. She had a stern look, her body movements showing she was clearly in charge.

I was sixteen-years-old at the time. It was ten p.m. on a Friday night and I had talked my friend Richie into taking me to see my fourteen-year-old sister, Denise, in the hospital. She had been diagnosed with scoliosis two years before; she had a severe 90-degree curve up her spinal column that a brace couldn't correct, so she needed surgery to straighten the curve. She was going to lie flat in bed for the next nine months; of course, I had to see Neasie! But I had to sneak in. Visiting hours were on Saturdays and Sundays only, from one to four p.m. Unfortunately, I had to work both those days as a waitress at the Continental restaurant in Cambridge. I was a junior in high school, and only could work weekends, so I planned to sneak in, see Neasie for the first time after her surgery.

Oh, how my heart ached for her! My little sister, she and I "the dividends" as my mother used to call us "the two children I never thought I'd have" as our mother Mary Connors used to say. So, of course, on that balmy April night I went to see Neasie.

Richie was hesitant, he said, "We have to sneak in, that's not a good idea and my dad let me borrow his car, I might not have it back in time, let's not go Kate." But I begged, pleaded with him. "Please, Richie," I said. "I only want to see Denise's face, know she's alive."

But as we approached the building, I wondered if I had made the right decision. The lights were out … doors were locked. But I had courage; I pressed the doorbell to her unit as perspiration appeared on my forehead. "Nerves," I said, "be brave, it's for Neasie."

I don't know if the pounding was real but I heard the heavy steps of the large nurse appearing, both the cap on her head and her feet appeared bigger than life. She opened the door slowly, looked at me intently. I said, "Sorry to be here so late but my sister had surgery, back surgery and I want to visit, her name is Denise Connors!"

The nurse looked at me, then at Richie. Her large frame suddenly softened, a smile appeared. "I'm sorry," she said, "the ward is quiet, Denise is asleep, and could you come back tomorrow?"

Tears came to my eyes. "No," I said, "I have to work, please let me in; I just need to know she's okay."

I wish I could remember her name. But this scary nurse, this wicked witch of the west transformed herself into the good witch, as in the Wizard of Oz. "Okay," she said, "be very quiet and only for a minute." I slowly walked inside. My shoes sounded heavy as I walked on my tiptoes, looking into each room as I passed; darkness, quiet and peaceful. The nurse hugged me as she showed me Denise's room.

"You're a good sister," she said. "Denise is lucky."

I could see the silhouette of Denise's body as the night-light shined on her. She was lying still, a back brace intact, and her breathing shallow. She looked so long and skinny, she had been through so much in the last two years. The doctors had stretched her body, literally put her on a board and pulled her spinal cord! Then a back brace for a year, hoping that would get rid of her curved spine. Instead, she was made fun of in school, laughed at and ridiculed. In the end the brace didn't work, her curved spine never improved. Finally the spinal fusion, the last resort.

I walked over and placed my hand on her shoulder, her head turned towards me, her green eyes slowly opened. "Neasie, it's me, Katie," I said. "I'm here."

I knew she thought it was a dream but she held my hand regardless. Denise looked over to her left side, towards the other bed that was occupied. She said, "That's Mary Beth, she had the same surgery as me." Mary Beth didn't stir, her stillness made me wonder if she was breathing. But then I noticed her cast covering her upper torso, the slow movement as she inhaled and exhaled. She almost looked angelic.

Something clicked that very moment, I wanted to help make Denise and Mary Beth better, heal their shattered bodies and make them laugh. Their little fourteen-year-old faces looked so needy, so vulnerable. I couldn't put words to my feelings that night as I left, but I knew I wanted to do more than just visit. I wanted to be part of that nurse's life, the lives of the sick and helpless, to make things better. I wanted those fourteen-year-old girls to be walking again and I wanted to be part of it. Thus, my thoughts of a nursing career began.

CHAPTER ONE

A Whole New World
May 1969

A cloud of black and white mortarboard caps momentarily blocked the sun and floated down as the warm spring air filled with a tumultuous roar, the exultant cheers of 400 graduating Waverly High School students. I was one of them. It was reality. I was seventeen-years-old, embarking on a career as a nurse and ready to leave high school behind. It had been a tough senior year, college boards, NLN's (National League for Nurses Exams) and trying to finish my senior year with a respectable grade.

The problem was I didn't get accepted into any R. N (Registered Nurse) programs or college level schools. So, I applied to several LPN (licensed practical nurse) programs and was admitted to all of them. I chose Shepard-Gill. Shepard-Gill, located on Newbury Street in Boston was an eighteen-month program that went right through the summer. Two prestigious women who were very successful within the nursing community ran the program.

So, in the midst of the Vietnam War, moratoriums and Woodstock, I headed to Newbury Street to enter a whole new world. I was frightened about leaving home, my safe nest, separation from my family and friends. My father teased me. "Kate, you'll be three miles from Waverly. What's the big deal?" The fact was I was scared to death! Was this what I really wanted? I was so uncertain! I think I would have preferred to work for a year then go to school. But I wasn't sure. My boyfriend of four years, Bill, was also leaving and joining the Marines. He was going to Basic Training that September. I would miss him and my predictable, comfortable life. Why did everything have to change? Yikes, I'm only 17; I don't want to grow up!

I remember in mid July my mother taking me to the bank "Okay, Katie," she said, "you need to withdraw some money, and you need to make the first tuition payment. You're going to school." I had argued with her for two weeks before on how I should wait, think it over, go to Woodstock with my sister Irene.

"No!" Mary Connors said. "You, young lady, are going to become a nurse!" God, did I hate her for about twenty seconds; her fiery green eyes were telling me I had no choice! Yikes again!

The middle of August we packed up my belongings and headed to Boston. My dad felt sad; he looked sort of guilty, possibly thinking maybe I should have taken the year off. He reached into his pocket; I heard the familiar sound of the change clinking around. The quarters were saying "give them to Katie." He dumped out all of his change, handed it over to me and said, "You better study. This is your last chance; call me to let us know how you're doing." My dad had been unhappy with my academic performance in high school. C's and B's. He started to give up on me, told me I liked to party too much. He was a Harvard graduate and wanted excellence from his children. I had been the disappointment in the family. As he handed me the change the look on his face said, "This is your last chance, don't screw up."

Newbury Street is a beautiful section of Boston, full of two-hundred-year-old buildings rich with history and character. As we walked into 22 Newbury, I marveled at the place, the high ceilings and mahogany banisters that led us up to my third floor dormitory room.

My roommate Trisha had already arrived. She was unpacking, placing her pictures on her bureau. I immediately noticed her boyfriend was a Marine. She proudly held his photo in front of her; I wondered if she was as homesick as I was feeling. I already missed my friends! I pictured my old hangouts: Friendly's, Victory Field, Palfrey Hill, I wanted to run back to my parents' car, back to my old life. Before I wimped out, Trisha started to tell me her boyfriend was in Vietnam, had been for six months. I knew at that moment I would stay in school, not run; if Trisha could do it so could I. I told myself to be brave; the sadness I was feeling would dissipate.

My mother, who had been lingering, stood up and decided to go. "OK Katie you'll be fine, toughen up; don't forget you're half Scottish." I looked at my dad, full of County Kerry, and tears came to both our eyes. He knew my thoughts, what I was feeling; he knew the Irish in me was stronger than ever. He hugged me and said, "You'll make a good nurse, just like your Aunt Teresa." I pictured my Aunt in her white uniform, her large frame lumbering around her house, taking care of my Uncle Frank as beads of sweat appeared on her forehead, her smiling at me and saying, "nursing is hard work, no money in it, your feet kill you at the end of the day, you truly have to love this profession to get into it."

I watched my parents walk down the steps and out to their car from my front window. The tears wouldn't stop. I went to my suitcase; lifted out my Rosary beads my godmother had given me for my confirmation. I put them in the pocket of my jeans, hoping the Blessed Mother would give me strength for the next twenty-four hours.

CHAPTER TWO

Reality

From the minute I started nursing school to the very last day it was nursing, nursing, and nursing! From one clinical rotation to the next we lived and breathed life and death illnesses and healing. The first three months were all academics of the nursing profession. I learned more about Florence Nightingale and her friends then I needed to know. We learned about the history of nursing, medicine, had a tour of Mass General hospital showing us the first nurse, first doctor and the first Operating Room, all adorning one wall of the hospital. Our academics included Nursing 101, Pharmacology, Microbiology, Anatomy and Physiology, and Music! Music? We all said "why?" Trisha and I laughed so hard when we found out we wouldn't graduate unless we passed music! Once a week, on Friday afternoons we had to sing as one of the instructors played the piano. The school dog, a little French poodle, would sit at the instructor's feet, probably laughing, not keeping a straight face like the rest of us.

This scenario was too much for my personality. My laughing fits and bad attitude almost got me thrown out of school. But I begged, pleaded and promised to sing and not laugh. I apologized for being immature; I did not want to face the wrath of my parents if I got tossed out of school, especially in the first month! My father had told me I was a risk and probably wouldn't stay in school, that's why my parents made me pay for the first half of my tuition. So I knew I couldn't screw up! I was learning so much in the first three months. While my homesickness would sneak back occasionally, I loved school and was too busy for my feelings to interfere with the learning process. I was intrigued with learning the function of every organ of the body and about diseases. How anyone stays healthy with all these illnesses, I thought. Pharmacology was my hardest subject; I always had trouble with math and I found it difficult to figure out dosages and formulas. But I had persevered and it started to become easy to me.

Boston could be a scary place too. I had grown up in suburbia and always had felt safe walking home late at night, but in Boston I felt I had to be with someone. Whether true or not, my imagination had bad people on every corner. I did feel safe in the cozy and student friendly pizza parlor across the street from school. My classmates and I would frequently go there for lunch or an early dinner. But come to find out there were drug deals going on … money being exchanged for marijuana, heroin and speed. I saw it at night from my large picture window and these longhaired men and women intrigued me, these bell bottomed entrepreneurs. Of course, it was a world foreign to me. I felt sorry for them, night after night exchanging money for drugs, sometimes the same people, and often time's new faces would appear.

One fall evening, about two months into school, I ran across the street to use the pay phone. I saw this young handsome guy, looking weird, paranoid, swiveling his head from side to side, as if someone was after him. I went into the pizza place to get a Coke first and then headed to the phone booth. Once inside I dialed my girlfriend Nancy's phone number. I had been talking for about thirty seconds when the young man started banging on the phone booth. "Get the fuck outta there," he said, several times. He was becoming more and more crazed looking, his eyes wild, pupils enlarged. I knew he was high on something. I hung up the phone and moved out. Slowly. A wonder, as I was almost paralyzed with fear!

"Who were you talking to on the phone about me, I'll fucking kill you," he snarled.

I still couldn't move, I prayed and then calmly said, "I was talking to my girlfriend. I wasn't talking about you."

He replied, "This is my fucking phone booth little girl, don't ever use it again."

"Okay, okay," I said as I walked away, and then started running. Fear propelled me, as I was never so frightened in my life.

That was my initiation into city life … a scary life of the late 1960s and early '70s. A world awash in new drugs, frightening drugs that brought a whole new meaning to "getting high." As I started my nursing career, I never realized how devastating this was going to be for our generation and the next thirty years.

CHAPTER THREE

Party Time

The homesickness I had experienced was gone, gone, gone! I was having so much fun I couldn't believe I had been missing home a mere three months before!

At Shepard-Gill, we had a curfew of seven p.m. Seventy students would get their pajamas on, talk, laugh, study, and hash over our day. My cheekbones would hurt from laughing so hard! I felt I was at a pajama party every night! Before a big exam we'd study for hours on end, sneak into the kitchen about 10 p.m. and eat! Eat! Eat! I put on fifteen pounds the first three months.

The continuous academic life was coming to an end. December was near and we had to move on to the hospitals we would be training at. Shepard-Gill affiliated with three large Boston hospitals, Massachusetts General, Beth Israel and New England Baptist. I was hoping to go to Mass General, a world-renowned facility with over one thousand in patient beds. But I found out two weeks before our "capping" that I was assigned to Beth Israel. The good news was my roommate Trisha would be joining me. More good news was that Beth Israel was up the street from Kenmore Square, a section of Boston with quite a bit of nightlife, bars and dancing. My eyes lit up when I heard the stories from the girls who graduated before me. "Go to K-K-K-Katie's or Lucifer's," one girl said, "These bars are great and the boys are hunks." Although I was excited about this new era in my life, a way of socializing, meeting new people, having fun, I knew I had to buckle down and study, continue to do well in school or I would have to face the wrath of my father. I was expected to be another Aunt Teresa.

I managed to pull off a B+ average, which was very good for me. I felt good about myself academically and knew I would succeed. I would miss the friends I made at Shepard-Gill as they headed off to different hospitals. I knew we would see one another, visit from time to time, but we'd miss the camaraderie we shared on Newbury Street.

It was the middle of December. I was packing, getting ready to go home for the holidays. I couldn't help noticing Trisha on her bed, tears in her eyes, looking at her boyfriend's picture. He had been in Nam for nine months; I put my hand on her shoulder and said, "Only three more months and he'll be home." I realized my boyfriend Bill was coming home from Paris Island soon. Being a Marine, he would be heading over to Vietnam. I could feel it; there would be no escaping it. Trisha brushed her hand over her boyfriend's picture and said, "He'll be okay." But we both knew that he might not be okay. My brother in-law, Paul, and some of his friends were in Nam, too, fighting, trying to stay alive. There had already been much causality, so we knew things might not be okay. I remember walking near the Prudential Center one sunny fall day. An Army nurse recruiter had a table outdoors and was recruiting nurses and encouraging future nurses to join the service, maybe go to Vietnam. I read through one of the pamphlets and how they made Army nursing sound so exciting! Go to war; help where you're really needed! But I was in such denial. I said to myself, this war would be over before I'm out of school. They don't need me. I was only eighteen not wanting to face death — the reality of the situation; but others were and I knew Bill would be over there soon.

So, we were "capped" on December 20th 1969. A capping is a ceremony that gives the student nurses a right of passage into the world of nursing, where she would embark on a new career of helping and healing. Candles were lit, caps were placed on our heads and I remember feeling so proud! The cap had a velvet blue ribbon across the front, signifying we were students; upon graduation, a black ribbon would replace the blue velvet.

My dad took me, some friends and family out to eat at a fancy restaurant after the ceremony and from there, a party at my house.

Two weeks later I was heading up Brookline Ave in my yellow Volkswagen towards Beth Israel; my car full of clothes, albums and pictures. I parked in front of the dorm, butterflies in my stomach, awaiting another change. I looked over at the hospital and realized I couldn't wait to take care of my first patient! A really sick person I could help back to wellness!

I was in awe of Beth Israel as I took a walk towards the hospital. Its building took up part of Brookline Ave abutting Massachusetts College of Art. I would be in Boston, one of the biggest medical Meccas in the world.

Beth Israel was founded in 1916 by the Boston Jewish Community to meet the needs of the growing Jewish immigrant population. It had over 500 in patient beds, largely made up of medical/surgical patients with a growing pediatric and obstetric unit as well as an Emergency Room. I looked over and saw an ambulance, its siren wailing, screech to a stop. The paramedics quickly rushed a patient into the Emergency Room. *God,* I thought, *I can't wait to get started, I just want to be part of this crazy, exciting world!*

I unloaded my car and attempted to pass the House Mother in the dormitory but she wouldn't let me by without a lecture. She was a middle-aged woman, who looked slightly disheveled and grumpy, but once she smiled at me, her personality changed. Her name was Maggie and she had been House Mother to nursing students "forever" as she put it. "Listen Sweetie," Maggie said, "the curfew is at 7 p.m. on weekdays, 11:30 p.m. on weekends, and I get cross if you disobey." I started to laugh. She said, "I can tell by the look in your eyes, you're going to try and break the rules."

I teased her back and said, "You know me already? Uh, you've been talking to my buddies back home?" We laughed together but I knew she wouldn't be an easy one to fool. She looked older than her fifty years; worn out, but she turned out to have a joyful spirit. When I loaded the elevator with all my belonging and was about to close the door, I saw Maggie flirting with the janitor, not a care in the world.

When I reached my dorm Trisha was already there and my girlfriend Sue. We didn't have to be in the hospital until Monday morning, in uniform to meet the administrative people at 7 a.m. Sue and Trisha looked nervous, anxious. I said, "Okay, guys. Get on your dancing shoes. We're going to K-K-K Katie's to go dancing!

Trisha said, "Oh, Katie, you're already starting. We should get ready for Monday."

"Oh, no," I repeated. "It's Saturday night we're going out." As we were leaving, I told Maggie we'd meet curfew."

"And if you don't?" she replied

"We'll be on time; God knows I don't want to deal with your Irish temper!" She only shook her head as she saw the three of us head to Kenmore Square. I remember my eighteen-year-old mind thinking I was totally ready for excitement, fun, challenges and risk taking (which I did best) and learning how to be a nurse. Nothing was going to stop me. Two mornings later, I was raring to go as I dressed in my starched uniform blue and white striped and a long white bib covering the uniform. And of course, a sweater, a blue sweater was mandatory with white nylons and white nursing shoes. Trisha told me to get the full affect of our $6-a-pair nylons (that helped the blood flow to our legs) we had to lay on the bed and keep our legs straight as we put them on. The two of us with our uniforms and white bibs, struggled, legs in the air trying to get these nylons on. I was laughing so hard and hoping no one would walk in and see our legs flailing in the air!

We met in a large solarium on one of the floors, being greeted by administrators and their welcoming committee. As the days went on with all these meetings the only thing that kept going through my head was let me take care of somebody, that's what I'm here for. I wanted to scream with frustration. But there was a whole week of meetings, introductions, rules and a tour of the hospital and finally our schedules for the following week. All the students would be starting out on medical surgical floors for the first three months and gradually move on to the different areas such as Pediatrics, Obstetrics and Psychiatry. By Friday night, I was ready to roll! "Okay, guys. K-K-K-Katie's again!" So, that was it, weekends in Kenmore Square, partying, some drinking but not getting out of control. Well not that out of control, at least we were always on foot.

By Monday, I couldn't wait. I was assigned to two patients. We had learned in our first clinical rotation about bed baths, bed making, (mitered corners girls!) taking blood pressures, a patient's pulse and respiration and ambulating with them. Looking back, I realized how slow moving this all was and how they stressed bed making! How tough can that be? The fun part was reading the patient's chart. That was a detailed account of their present illness, past medical and surgical history and something about their personal life if necessary. I spent two hours the night before reading my patients' charts and jotting down appropriate information. I was so excited I could barley sleep the night before!

CHAPTER FOUR

"Fraanc"

The first patient I was assigned to was fifty-five-year-old Frank, only he pronounced it "Fraanc" with a French accent. I distinctly knew his real name was Frank. He had to be from the North End of Boston and was very Italian, but I let him think I believed he was "Fraanc" from Paris. Didn't he know his dripping gold chains were a dead giveaway?! Anyway, "Fraanc" had had a heart attack, damaged one of his coronary arteries and was now in the healing process. He had already been in the hospital a week, was ready for discharge when he developed chest pain again; was sent to the coronary care unit where the doctors ruled out another heart attack and sent him back to the regular medical floor. That's where I came in. I was his student nurse until discharge.

I was instructed to help with his personal care, take his vital signs and follow-up on all other doctors' orders under my instructor's supervision. The first two days went well; I made his bed, took his blood pressure every two hours, gave him a back rub and offered support. "This is a breeze," I said to Trisha. "He's a nice guy, easy to take care of." But the next day "Fraanc" was waiting for me, said he didn't feel well, was too tired to "wash up."

Um, I said to myself. *Not according to the report I received from the night nurse. She said he was fine, slept all night.* I said, "Okay, Fraanc, I'll report this to the charge nurse, or your doctor right now." I had already taken his vital signs and he was stable.

"No," he said. "Just get me a basin and I'll wash up." So, I proceeded with the daily routine, placed the basin with hot soapy water in front of him with the face cloth and towel and started to leave the room. He called to me. "Katie, I really need help, please wash me." He preceded to hand me the face cloth and pulled down the sheet where he was totally naked … genitals exposed. He pointed and said, "Please, wash me."

I started to stutter. "Fr-Fr-Frank, I need to ask my instructor," and I backed out the room, turning totally red. I caught my instructor before she headed into another patient's room and told her the story.

"Do you think he's capable of washing himself?" she asked.

"Yes," I said. "I don't want to go near him."

My instructor came back into his room with me, retook his vital signs and pronounced him healthy enough to wash his own groin. In her kind, firm way she told "Fraanc" to back off and stop trying to take advantage of an eighteen-year-old nursing student. Things were never the same between Frank and I. I'd catch him leering at me, winking, making me feel uncomfortable. It was 1969 and sexual harassment was in no one's vocabulary. I breathed a sigh of relief two days later when he was discharged.

My second patient was a lady who will always remain in my heart. Her name was Mary Hill. Little did I know at the time I would be taking care of her again during one of her several admissions within the next year.

Mary was fifty-years-old, divorced, the mother of three loving grown children, two boys and a girl. Mary had found a lump on her breast and was in the hospital to be "worked up", meaning blood tests, mammogram and probably a biopsy. I introduced myself and she was thrilled to have a student. She was nervous, apprehensive and in need of someone to talk to. I was that link. I proceeded to write down her medical and surgical history, which consisted of three normal vaginal deliveries of her children and an UGI series (upper gastrointestinal) the month before because of continued nausea and stomach discomfort. All tests came back negative; the doctors found nothing wrong.

The next day when I saw her she said, "The lump is suspicious. They are going to do a biopsy." Mary went to the operating room about 9 a.m. Two hours later, she was back, the preliminary results didn't look hopeful but the doctor was waiting for the final pathology report. He wanted her to think about surgery. Mary was crying when I went into her room. It was the first time in my life I felt helpless; there was nothing I could do to make her better. Her daughter came into the room to visit. She was not much older than me, maybe twenty. She was full of hope for her mother. How would I feel if that was my mom?

When I left the hospital that day I needed to be alone. A light snow was falling as I headed down Brookline Ave. With just a sweater on, I thought of my mother saying, "Katie, get a coat on, you'll catch a cold" or when I was little I'd come in from a wintry day, having just built a snowman with my sister Denise, our cheeks all rosy, our mittens frozen with icicles hanging off them; our hands would be so cold we'd cry. My mother would slowly take our mittens off and gently rub our hands and put them under her "wings" her arms, until we had warmed up. Oh! How I had taken all that tenderness, caring and love for granted. I sat on a bench, put my head in my hands and just cried. I cried for Mary, her daughter, her sons and how life can be so unfair.

When I got back to the dorm, I called my mother. I heard her cheery voice, her singsong voice, "Hello!" I could feel her sadness as I told her about Mary. This was the first time I realized my mother could get sick, she could die. Somehow, I thought of my mother above everyone else, she'd never get sick; mothers don't die. But she was vulnerable like everyone else; she could be Mary in that bed. I went to sleep that night more appreciative of my mom, and the things I had.

It was Friday, the end of February when a bunch of us ventured to Lucifer's, another bar in Kenmore Square. None of us were twenty-one and we all had either our older sister's IDs or fake ones. There were no picture licenses at the time so we could get away with it. We had a curfew of course, but the few hours we had helped relieve the tension of the previous week.

The six of us joined a table of guys about twenty minutes after we got there. The boys were students at Boston University and Boston College. It was a festive and fun two hours. We felt cohesiveness, a coming together after a long week of school. One of the guys I was talking to was twenty-five; he was a medical student at BU, wanted to become a surgeon. I talked to him for over an hour, told him about my patients, and had him laughing when I told him about "Fraanc". "This guy is so mature," I told Trisha on the way home. "How am I going to stay faithful to Bill?"

Trisha replied, "Face it, Katie, you're not." We both laughed. But the fact was I felt guilty. I was home, getting an education, having fun while Bill was over in Vietnam, not knowing if he would see the next twenty-four hours. Trisha said, "Kate, you're eighteen. Live your life, give yourself permission to have fun." So, I did my best; I tried anyway, but I was growing up, moving away from the past. I was at a crossroads in my life, I wanted more; I deserved more. So I gave myself permission to live my life, have fun as a nursing student, work hard and reward myself. No harm in that.

CHAPTER FIVE

Moving On

The spring days of April arrived. It was 1970. Boston was starting to blossom. Trees were budding and the crocuses were appearing. I loved school, loved nursing; I was happy in my new life. But I had no money. I took on the responsibility and ownership of my sister Kerry's car. It was a yellow Volkswagen and I would have to pay $90 a month. My savings were dwindling. I called my dad on a Friday night to tell him my dilemma. His reply was, "Go to work."

I said, "Dad, I'm in school."

"Yeah. So?" he said. "You have a B+ average, your teachers told me you could work in the hospital as a nursing assistant if you maintain a B average. Get a job, Kate."

I wanted to kill my father! I hung up the phone on him and yelled, "Cheapo!" In years to come, I thanked my dad for what he did. It was one of life's lessons about responsibility and not depending on someone else's money.

The following Monday I went to the nursing office at Beth Israel, got a job as a nursing assistant and started the following week. My schedule was busy. I had clinical practice for school three days a week, two full days of classes, then I went to work on those two days as an aide, plus one day over the weekend. The nurses on the floor gave me more responsibility because I was a student. My shift was three p.m. to nine p.m. on one of the surgical floors. After the patients had their surgery and spent a few hours in the recovery room, they would arrive on my floor. I loved this job! I listened and learned; my brain was like a sponge. I absorbed everything the nurses and doctors taught me and never forgot. There were also medical patients on the floor, those who didn't have surgery but needed to be hospitalized for medical reasons, such as strokes and heart attacks.

A patient I remember was Lilly, an 83-year-old lady who had a CVA (cerebral vascular accident) or better known as a stroke. A CVA is when a clot forms and goes to the brain; a hemorrhage occurs or even a spasm that narrows the blood flow. Lilly was an active 83-year-old who was driving every day. She had been having occasional numbness and tingling in her hands and feet but ignored the symptoms. What she was experiencing were "TIAs" or "trans ischemic attacks" — little strokes cutting off oxygen and blood supply to the brain for a short period of time, but the symptoms would come back.

Lilly had been out to lunch with her two girlfriends at a local restaurant when suddenly she stopped talking, her mouth started to droop and she couldn't move her right arm. Her friends called an ambulance. I took care of Lilly for two weeks before she died. She would stare up at me with her big brown frightened eyes, unable to speak, communicate or turn over in her bed by herself. She was totally dependent on the nurses for her care. Lilly was so tiny I could care for her alone, turn and position her in bed, clean her up when she messed the bed.

I felt helpless, no matter what I did or the doctors did I knew Lilly would die. After only seven months of school, I was beginning to accept death, remembering from my Catholic upbringing that God has a greater plan for us all. Growing up I was used to my parents going to wakes, especially my dad. I remember him coming home one night from a wake in a really good mood, whistling. I said, "Dad, someone just died. Why are you so cheerful? Aren't you sad?"

"Kate," he said, "Mr. O'Toole was eighty-five. He had a great life. It's a celebration, and he's in heaven now."

Somehow I couldn't imagine being so joyful, but I'd glimpse at my father reading the death notices in the *Boston Globe*, the "Irish Sports Page," looking for friends and acquaintances who had passed on.

Lilly died while I was at supper the following night. I didn't get to say goodbye. She experienced another massive stroke and no heroics were performed. This was the first death of a patient for me. I was afraid to be in the room alone with her and I wasn't quite sure why. I kept thinking she would breathe again, and when I'd look over at her I thought I'd see her take in a breath; it was my imagination.

When I was little my brothers used to tell me to look up at the wall when I was lying in bed and I would see my grandmother (who had died years before) in the dark. Her face would be on the wall. "Spirits come back," my brother, John, would say. My sister, Denise, and I would lie in bed shaking, scared to death, thinking we were seeing Grammie. My brothers would be laughing at us in the other room.

I looked over at Lilly and wondered where her spirit was. Could it still be in the room? Suddenly one of the nurses walked in the room, startled me and I screamed "Ahhh!"

She in turn screamed "Ahhh," back. We both stood in stunned silence, staring at each other, and then we started to laugh.

"Meg," I said, "you startled me. I thought you were Lilly's spirit."

Meg said to me, "Is this the first death for you?"

"Yeah," I said, "my first."

Meg replied, "It takes time, Kate. You'll get used to it."

"My Aunt Theresa told me that when a person dies, their soul leaves their body through their feet," I said to Meg, hoping for a response.

Meg had a smile on her face; she was a seasoned nurse and had probably seen more than she'd care to remember. She was packing up Lilly's belongings, emptying her drawers and throwing different items away when she replied, "I think that is an old tale our grandparents believed, something to make them feel better when a loved one dies, that their soul travels to somewhere special."

We had to wait for Lilly's family to arrive before post mortem care could be done. Her kids needed to say their goodbyes, clear her room and get her belongings. The head nurse never made me do postmortem care with Meg. Fortunately, they knew I was upset. After all, this was my "first."

CHAPTER SIX

Getting Comfortable

As the months passed, I became more comfortable with all aspects of health care. Sickness and death came with the territory of being a nurse, and when patients got well, recovered from surgery you felt as if you were part of the healing process. I no longer cringed at the sight of open wounds or blood, no longer gagged at certain bodily fluids, and I learned to communicate with stroke victims when they couldn't speak. My legs would ache at the end of a shift, after running around on the floors, answering call lights, emptying bed pans, changing dressings, getting people in and out of bed all day; the ache in my back was a good ache after a day's work, a day of accomplishments and satisfaction.

My grades were good. I loved Anatomy and Physiology, wanted to learn more and more, not like in high school. I found something I could do and do it well. I cared about my patients. The nurses on the floors, my fellow students and even Maggie, the housemother, became my family. I met so many people from all walks of life; it was an eye opener a definite learning experience.

There was a classmate of mine, an adorable petite Jewish girl named Barbara, who knew everything! She was a few years older than me, beautiful, knowledgeable and sophisticated. I loved talking to her because she was so worldly! We were on a clinical rotation together when she told me her real reason for becoming a nurse … to find a Jewish doctor. My eyes widened! "You know what you want already?" I asked.

"Yes," she said. "I'll get what I want." She told me the way to a man's heart (particularly a Jewish man's heart) was to be seductive and sexy, make them think they are the most important people on Earth! None of this had ever entered my mind. Barbara said, "Don't you want a rich husband? Or haven't you thought about it?"

"No," I said, "I just got out of high school." She told me you had to walk a certain way — a "sexy" way — and she grabbed my hand and brought me to the utility room. And in her long blue nurse's uniform, bib and all, she transformed herself into a sexy-looking older woman. She pursed her lips, threw her chest out and swayed her hips. I was mesmerized.

She said, "Okay. Now you try it." So, I imitated Barbara, practicing for ten minutes. I knew I looked stupid, it just wasn't my style to purse my lips and swing my hips to look sexy. But I never forgot that day, an initiation into the world of finding a husband.

Two weeks later, the beginning of May, I finished working on a particularly difficult floor. I was exhausted after taking care of a man who had a gunshot wound in his abdomen. The bullet went right through his gut and somehow damaged his spinal cord. Hence, he was paralyzed. When I took care of him he was four days post-operative after removing the bullet. He was thirty-five-years-old, from a tough section of town, had been at the wrong place at the wrong time and ended up with a bullet in his spine that was meant for someone else.

His name was Max. He had two small children and a wife who wasn't dealing with his accident very well. It was overwhelming and she was still in a state of shock; she also couldn't deal with Max's anger. He would scream at us as we turned and positioned him in bed. Scream at his wife for no reason at all. He was a tough patient to have to care for, physically and emotionally. I wanted to support his wife as well. I listened to her vent her feelings and cry and scream. I was new at this and didn't know how to respond, so I just held her hand and shook my head in understanding, listening to her every word and validating her feelings. Max eventually left the hospital and was transferred to a rehabilitation facility. I never heard from him or his wife again.

I headed back to my dormitory the night after taking care of Max. I went straight to my mailbox hoping to receive a letter from Bill. He had been in Vietnam for three months; it had been three weeks since I'd heard from him. *Weird*, I thought as I opened and shut my empty mailbox. I called my parents when I got to my room. When my dad answered, I asked if I had any letters from Bill.

"No," he said hesitantly. The country knew that the war in Vietnam was getting worse. More and more casualties each day; the whole war sucked! Why were we there anyway? I told my father I'd be home for the weekend and Trisha would be with me.

The next day, Trisha and I jumped into my Volkswagen and headed west onto Storrow Drive. I had a restless, uneasy feeling about Bill and I was going to call his family when I got home. As I turned my car onto Longmeadow Road, heading toward my house, I saw Richie, Bill's brother, parked in front of my house. Something was wrong. I walked in the front door and looked at Rich and my parents sitting solemnly on the couch, awaiting my arrival. Rich said, "Bill's been hurt. He stepped on a mine and lost his leg."

I was shocked and didn't want to believe what I had heard. "Why, why, why?" I screamed as I heaved one of my shoes through my parent's window, shattering the glass all over the floor. I fell on my knees, put my face in my hands and cried. Cried for Bill, for the senseless war and all the pain, injuries, and deaths it was causing.

Two months later, I went to visit Bill at Philadelphia Naval Hospital along with his two brothers. The doctors, nurses and support staff were helping young men, all injured from the war, back to reality. I looked around at these young men, some of them not even twenty-years-old, their fresh wounds, the look of hopelessness and despair in their eyes, and the nurses who arrived each shift to help them heal physically, mentally and spiritually.

What I noticed most about the staff was how they projected hope, their wonderful attitude and sense of humor. They wouldn't let their patients give up; they helped the soldiers see that they would get better, the pain would go, depression would dissipate and they would be home with their families soon. My eyes never left these nurses who encountered new casualties every day and how they bravely did their jobs, bringing light and love to all these men.

I went back to school after visiting Bill and was never quite the same. Nursing suddenly seemed like an awesome responsibility. I realized to be a good nurse you had to heal the body, mind and spirit in order for the patients to get well, a balancing act. I tried to describe to my colleagues and staff nurses what the veteran's hospital was like, and the responsibility of the doctors and nurses as wounded men would arrive everyday. But it was so tragic it was almost indescribable. Even now, thirty years later, I remember those nurses, their healing hands, open hearts and positive attitudes.

CHAPTER SEVEN

Dog Days of Summer

Hot August days. Wartime. Moratoriums. Four months to go until graduation. The humidity was unbearable as we left our dorm and headed to the Boston Common to be part of the moratorium, which is a peace rally, a group of people making a statement against the Vietnam War, a get together of like-minded people. The pungent smell of marijuana pervaded the air as longhaired men and women, in bell-bottoms and love beads chanted, "No Nam" and prayed for peace. A demonstration to show the president they wanted the country out of Vietnam; these Americans wanted Nixon to take them seriously. Speeches were made, people held up placards with the names of the dead on them as candles were lit and church bells tolled.

The moratorium was on national TV that night, and as I watched it I had such mixed feelings. I wanted to believe our men were over there fighting for a reason. If not, why did Bill lose his leg? But yet, it felt wrong; thousands were dying.

I felt depressed after watching the news and decided to go over to the hospital and see if any of the floors needed help. As I learned later in nursing, that was a dumb question; they always need help! When I went to my favorite surgical floor and asked the charge nurse if she needed some assistance, she looked at me and said, "Is the Pope Catholic?" I ran back to the dorm and changed my clothes, and fifteen minutes later, I was giving back rubs, changing dressings and trying to make sick people laugh. That was how I dealt with my personal problems at the time; I escaped into someone else's problems. I was aware of what I was doing, but said to myself, *If I'm not here I'd be at K-K-K-Katie's drinking!*

When I went back to the dorm at 11 p.m., I heard hysterical laughter coming from one of the rooms. I walked down the hall to see what was so funny! About four of my fellow students had a sphygmometer (blood pressure machine) and they were taking each other's blood pressure and laughing hysterically! I sat on the bed trying to figure out what was so amusing. Then I realized they were all stoned! I laughed and said, "You guys smokin' some good shit?"

Lori beamed and said, "Watch the mercury go down when I take Kim's blood pressure. It's intense!" So, I watched, they killed themselves laughing. I was having more fun watching them crack up, and I was not stoned!

As I walked back to my room, I laughed and thought the four of them would have enjoyed Boston Common and that marijuana was very much alive in campuses all over the country. What was so appealing about marijuana? It loosened a person up after a busy day; the drug brought peacefulness to the psyche that alcohol couldn't do. More and more people were choosing pot over alcohol. Some of pot's appeal was its illicit status. There were campaigns going on for its legalization but it still seemed a far way off and the government was strict in certain instances. In July of 1969, a twenty-year-old former high school track star got twenty years in a Virginia jail — the minimum sentence for drug possession —exactly the same for first-degree murder. Legalization definitely was not in the forefront of the Nixon Administration.

CHAPTER EIGHT

Nearing the End

"The last two innings of the game." That's what my father used to say as something was ending, finishing. It was the beginning of November and I would be graduating in two months. I was trying to figure out where I was going to apply for jobs and if I wanted to move back home or get an apartment. I was feeling restless one day and decided to go visit my classmates at Massachusetts General Hospital and then go to the New England Baptist another day to see if either of these institutions appealed to me.

I went solo. Hopped on the train and headed over to the General. As the train stopped, I could see the world-renowned hospital from my window. People came from all over the world to get treated here. I had phoned my friend Marilyn at her dorm and told her I'd be there around 11 a.m. She greeted me at the elevator and said, "Guess who I took care of?"

"Ummm," I said, "let me guess, one of the Kennedy's?" Then I quickly replied, "Of course not, they go to the Baptist. Who? Marilyn, maybe another well-known political family?"

"No," she said. "Derek Sanderson." Okay, I knew the name, knew it was sports related, but I couldn't connect. My mother would kill me! She was "sooo" into all athletes. Then I remembered, hockey, Bruins, long dark hair.

"Cool, Marilyn. What happened to him?"

"I'm not sure," she said, "orthopedics related."

I said, "Marilyn, I thought you took care of him?"

"Well, actually, I walked by his room. Valerie took care of him."

I shook my head and we laughed. "Take me on a tour," I said.

Mass. General was founded in 1811. It is the third largest hospital in the United States and the oldest and largest in New England. It has over eight hundred inpatient beds offering diagnostic and therapeutic care in every specialty of medicine and surgery. It has a large hospital based research program with over a two million dollar budget. It is also the largest teaching hospital of Harvard Medical School … definitely impressive.

Marilyn and I wandered around the hospital floors; she showed me where she had been working and I met some of her patients. Marilyn had a great sense of humor and kept me laughing all day. Mass. General Hospital seemed to treat many celebrities and more fascinating people than other Boston hospitals, but of course, they were always under alias names. Movie stars were in and out of the General, arriving in sunglasses, leaving with sunglasses and kerchiefs as the rumors went. A bunch of us sat around Marilyn's dorm room wondering what these "movie stars" had done. "Face lifts," said Gina.

"Tummy tucks and butt lifts," stated Wendy. We could only speculate and guess, but it was fun imagining.

I felt a new world open to me that day, yet I wasn't sure if I was ready for such a large hospital or living in Boston. I was goal oriented though. My plan was to work two years and then go back to school to get my R.N. and Bachelor's degree. I felt driven. *Why didn't I study in high school?* I thought. *If I had done well, I would have gone directly to an RN program; it would have been much easier.*

On the train back to Beth Israel, I realized it didn't matter. I was learning, having fun, meeting new people, and in a few months, I'd be a practical nurse! I felt proud of myself and would accomplish something, making my parents happy, something I had never done in the past. I had somehow felt I always disappointed them. My dad was still mad at me for doing poorly in high school and not getting into a good college. But as the train moved back and forth side to side I realized not all of what happened was my fault.

My home life, as loving as it could be was dysfunctional, crazy at times. I lived in day-to-day fear of my problematic brother and a father who demanded excellence from his children. He had been so poor growing up, worked his way to the top, a Harvard graduate, and expected the same from us. His bouts of alcoholism interfered. I would see my father sober for months, sometimes years, then suddenly he'd start drinking again, go on a bender for no rhyme or reason; I always felt I had done something to make him start drinking, I didn't realize that that is what alcoholism was. But I loved him, knew he only wanted the best for me, for my siblings. I now had the opportunity to improve my life, make something of myself and I was finding being a nurse was the missing link; I felt at home on these hospital floors, nurturing people back to health, being kind and caring to family members and feeling good after a long day's work.

I had high hopes for myself that day and decided to put in an application at Mass. General and Beth Israel, just in case I wanted to work in Boston. When I went home the following week I would check out hospitals closer to home. Things would fall into place.

CHAPTER NINE

Graduation, 1970

In early December, after finishing classes, I headed over to the hospital to work the 3-9 p.m. shift. The patient I took care of that night was Mary Hill, one of the first patients I had cared for that year. She was dying. Since I had last seen her, she'd had a mastectomy (breast removal) but the cancer had spread and there was no hope for survival. Her once pretty figure and weight of 140 pounds was down to 85 lbs. Her cheeks were sunken in and she had the odor of death and cancer eating away at her slim frame.

She had developed an infection in the remaining breast tissue and was draining copious amounts of fluid from the breast. She was in pain, especially when I was changing her dressing. We both cried when she told me she knew she was dying. "I only want to live until Christmas. My daughter is pregnant and her due date is December 25. I want to be a grandmother before I die," Mary said. I prayed on my way home she'd last three more weeks.

Our graduation was December 21st at the John Hancock Hall in Boston. We all looked beautiful. That's what I said to my classmates as we entered the hall, laughing and joyous! We were radiant in white nurse's uniforms and our caps. The ceremony was short, to the point, and our ribbons were changed from blue to black on our nurse's caps. After the ceremony, my dad took us out to eat and back to my house for a big celebration with the rest of my family and friends. Back at the house my brother John cornered me and asked me when I was going back to school for my R.N. "A couple of years," I said.

"Bad move," said my brother, "you should go back soon or you never will."

My father chimed in and gave his two cents worth in agreement with my brother. Finally, I said, "Guys, could I enjoy tonight? I've been a nurse for about two seconds." *Typical family shit!* I said to myself as I ran up the stairs into my room. I wanted peace and quiet for five minutes while I called Mary Hill's floor. I was anxious to see if she was still alive. The nurse at the desk told me she was hanging in there. Her son was with her and her daughter had the baby that morning. I was so happy ... my prayers were answered!

I took two weeks off before I started my new job. I took a position at a community hospital local to my parents; I planned to live at home in hopes of saving some money. Plus, I had to pass the state boards in another month and didn't want any added stress.

In the middle of January, I started my orientation at the hospital. I was assigned a preceptor who showed me the ropes. I realized how much I missed school, my friends, Beth Israel and Boston! I wanted my dorm life back! Unfortunately, it was time to move on, grow up.

My floor was mostly neurosurgery ... brain tumors removed or spinal surgeries. There were many cancer patients as usual and once they were discharged from the hospital, I never knew what happened to them; that was the part I hated. I had taken care of them, helped them to recovery and then they were discharged, without me ever knowing if the cancer reoccurred or even if they were still alive. I also took care of many medical patients with neurological diseases such as multiple sclerosis, guillian-barre and myasthenia gravis, which are all life-threatening illnesses. The scary ones to me were the patients with meningitis, brain tumors and viral infections affecting normal brain functions.

One of the patients on my floor was a sixty-year-old professor who suddenly developed some type of brain lesion. At first, the doctors didn't know if it was a viral or bacterial infection so they started him on a course of intravenous antibiotics that didn't help at all. His symptoms worsened and he slowly became confused and disoriented. He needed a private duty nurse after a while because he required so much care. What was frightening to me was one day he was fine, teaching a class in Economics, and the next day he was hospitalized and getting progressively worse. Nothing was helping, even the surgery he had didn't help, one complication arose after another and his nurse worked her tail off.

The private nurse he had worked twelve-hour days seven days a week, her name was Marie. She was middle-aged, large framed with flowing dyed blonde hair and her cap neatly placed on her head. I never saw her sit or stop working in those twelve-hours. She was feisty, too! She told the doctors what to do and was a real patient and family advocate. I never saw her take a day off. I looked up to her. One weekend when I was helping her turn Mr. Brookes, I said, "Marie, do you ever take a day off?"

She said, "I work seven days a week for nine months straight then I take three months off." Marie worked for an agency and was not an employee of the hospital. She was paid by the family, so she was able to do this.

I said, "Aren't you tired? Don't you want a day off, a social life?"

She laughed. "This building is my social life. Besides, I'm going on a three-month cruise pretty soon."

Mr. Brookes died of a brain abscess one week later. Marie asked me if I would help her do post-mortem care. I was hesitant and thought of my first patient, Lilly, who had died a year before. But I gathered strength and helped Marie. It felt so impersonal as we wrapped him in a shroud and put nametags on his hands and feet. I felt as if he wasn't a person as I watched Marie turn him, clean him up and finally close his eyes. What I was doing was learning to detach from death and realize this was part of life, part of being a nurse.

After working on the neurological floor for a year, I realized I needed a change. I applied for a few different jobs on different floors but they were looking for permanent night nurses. I didn't want to leave the hospital, yet I wasn't happy doing that type of nursing. I was also becoming restless living at home. My parents were great, but if I stayed, I'd have to live under their rules in their structured life.

One morning, on my day off, I got up at 7 a.m. to use the bathroom. When I went to go back to bed, my bed was made. I said, "Mom, it's my day off. I was going back to sleep."

She said, "Oh, well. Sorry. Don't waste your day sleeping."

I realized I needed to move.

CHAPTER TEN

Another Change

My sister Irene lived in the Clarendon Hill Apartments in Sutton with her husband, Paul, and son, Pauly. She told me I could live with them; use the extra bedroom if I needed a change. About a month later, I quit my job and moved in with Irene and family. I considered this temporary but I loved living with them!

I applied for a job at Mass General and started working there six-weeks later on an orthopedic floor. The bad part was I had a day/night rotation. I would work 7 a.m. to 3 p.m. for two weeks, then 11 p.m. to 7 a.m. for two weeks, a schedule that was disruptive to you physically and emotionally. Yuck! I knew I hated the night shift but I took the job in hopes of getting on the day shift eventually, plus it would be a great learning experience.

My social life had been uneventful living at my parents. Bill and I had broken up soon after I finished school. We hung in there, trying to make our relationship work but it wasn't meant to be. I was twenty years old and ready for a new job; meeting new people and I knew MGH would be a learning experience.

I took the bus, then subway from Sutton into Boston every day to get to work. Some mornings were grueling trying to get there on time. I had an assistant head nurse on the day shift who took a disliking to me; for whatever reason. If I showed up at 7:10 a.m. she'd harass me, lecture me about being on time. So, I'd get up even earlier and try to catch the bus leaving Sutton at 6 a.m. to make it on time. But for some reason, I was always ten or fifteen minutes late and of course, "Nurse Ratchet" was on my case. One day in early May, she put me on warning and said if I were late again she'd report me to Administration. I was nervous and couldn't relax the night before work, worrying I wouldn't get there on time.

I caught the 5:50 a.m. bus the next morning so I would be sure to be on time. The bus was headed to Lechmere Square and I would catch the train to MGH. Wrong. The bus broke down, it was 6:20 a.m. and I had to get to work!

"Yikes," I said, "I might lose my job." So, in full uniform, pocketbook in hand, I scurried off the bus and stuck my thumb out to hitchhike. A middle-aged man stopped immediately. I looked in the window and said, "I need a ride to MGH and I have to be there by 7 a.m. or I'll lose my job."

"No problem, hop in," he said. I checked him out and he seemed like a gentleman (maybe). He talked to me about his family, kids, grandkids and I told him about Nurse Ratchet. I had him laughing as he drove me to the front door of the hospital, it was 6:50 a.m. As I was thanking him and opening the door, he said, "Before you leave, could I touch your white nylons? (He was leering at my thighs.) I've never been this close to a nurse before."

"Oh, no," I said. "This is throw-up time. Go buy yourself a pair of nylons, you pervert," and I lunged out of the car. So, he was a dirty old man after all, another "FRAANC." I ran into the lobby of Mass

General with a sigh of relief, glad to be safe, out of the car and ON TIME!

I had a love/hate relationship with the night shift. I couldn't sleep during the day and went to work most nights exhausted. My nephew, Paul, was two years old and when I got home from work at eight in the morning I would try to sleep, but the sound of "Sunny Days" from Sesame St. or "It's a Beautiful Day in the Neighborhood" from our friend, Mr. Rogers, would keep me awake. So, I'd cat nap and go into work at 11 p.m. needing a good night's sleep. I learned so much on the night shift, though, and the nurses were great. Being on an orthopedic floor, I would see so many car accident victims who had broken bones and needed surgical intervention.

One night, I took care of a 30-year-old man named Tim who had been in a motorcycle accident. He had broken his hip and the doctors were going to do surgery the following Monday. In the meantime, they put him in "bucks traction." This type of traction immobilizes the limb for a period of time so there would be no more damage. I took care of Tim before and after his surgery. He was a challenging patient because he was very active in his personal life and didn't like to be lying in bed. He missed being on the road and missed his motorcycle. He was restless and jumpy and couldn't go through an eight-hour shift without yelling at someone.

Two days after his surgery, I was working the night shift when he put his call light on at about 2 a.m. When I went into his room, he told me he was short of breath. I took his vital signs; B/P 120/70, heart rate 120, respirations were 28, no temperature. I knew his heart and respiration rates were elevated and immediately called one of the residents on call. The doctor arrived five minutes later, and Tim was now having chest pains. I ran and got a portable oxygen tank and administered 3 liters.

Twenty minutes later, a chest X-ray revealed a pulmonary embolus. Evidently, Tim developed a blood clot in his leg after surgery and a part of that clot broke off and went to the right lower lobe of his lung. This is a very serious and life-threatening trauma, but Tim turned out okay! We started him on intravenous heparin (a blood thinner) and transferred him to the Intensive Care Unit where the nurses could monitor him more closely.

I remember pushing his bed down the long corridor with two other doctors to the ICU. He was being monitored by an EKG (cardiogram) machine, and with the oxygen going through his nostrils, his IV flowing in, he looked scared to death. He grabbed my hand when I was leaving and said, "I'm scared shitless." Tim recovered and in five days, he was back on my floor giving the nurses a hard time.

I had been working at the General for three months. Working nights was not getting better and there was no end in sight. I had to do another year of nights before I would be considered for permanent days. I told myself to stick it out — it would get better. But an incident that happened one night made me rethink working this shift. Although the incident was funny, hilarious to many, it was an occurrence that helped me look at my job in a different light.

At the end of the night shifts, probably around 5 a.m., I'd get exhausted and force myself to function for the next two hours. One morning at 5:30, one of the nurses asked me to help her out in the four-bed ward. She asked me to take all the vital signs (blood pressure, pulse, respiration and temperature) on the patients. As I headed in the room, she said, "Oh, yeah. They all need rectal temperatures."

I entered the room, washed my hands and approached each bed. They were all asleep so I decided to place the thermometer in each person then go back and finish the vital signs. I inserted the rectal thermometer in the first without a peep from him, washed my hands and did the same for the second and third patient. All had thermometers right at the bedside. When I approached the fourth patient, there was no thermometer so I went and got one.

When I returned he groggily looked at me and kept blinking, trying to wake up. *Boy is he young. I wonder what's wrong with him.* I thought. I noticed he had only a T-shirt on, no hospital gown, which is unusual. I said to him in a whisper, "Roll over, I need to take your temperature." He obediently rolled over and I heard him snoring as I inserted the rectal thermometer. I went back to the other three patients, finished their vital signs, recorded them and headed back to bed four. When I got there, he was sitting up in bed, holding the thermometer and laughing.

"Hi," he said, "I'm Dr. Johnson, one of the residents." And teasingly said, "I was taking a nap until someone started poking at me." The big grin on his face didn't make me feel less embarrassed; I turned red as a tomato. "It's okay," he said. "I needed a good laugh; this place is much too serious." Dr. Johnson was on call and thought he'd catch a couple of hours sleep until his beeper interrupted him; instead, I interrupted him! By 7 a.m., the staff on the floor knew the story and I avoided Dr. Johnson at all costs.

One doctor was laughing and said, "So, you got to do a rectal on Bob Johnson. Good for you!"

"Ha … ha … real funny," I said, not finding the humor the rest of the staff did in this incident. Although weeks later I realized it was pretty funny, I knew nights was getting to me and my exhaustion was starting to impair my decision-making. Furthermore, I was too tired to care.

CHAPTER ELEVEN

Spring Fever

The Boston Common ... blossoming trees, lush green grass, swan boats. I felt so alive, fertile, a lust for life that spring. I was in the Common after work, met my boyfriend George whom I had been dating for a couple of months. We were tossing a Frisbee around and enjoying the early evening balmy weather. Everyone seemed so happy, so alive; springtime in Boston.

As we continued to toss the Frisbee, George told me he was leaving for Colorado for three weeks the end of May, beginning of June. "Do you want to go Kate? I'm driving my van with two other guys to Colorado Springs." One of the guys was going on a mountain climbing expedition and George thought it would be a good opportunity to travel. Two girls I knew from high school were also going.

"Tempting," I said to George, "but I just started this job and I'd never get vacation time, never mind three weeks."

The next day when I went to work, "Nurse Ratchet" was on my case again for something different, something stupid as far as I was concerned. She clearly had resentments towards me. But why? Maybe I looked like someone she hated in the past. Regardless, I tried to be friendly to her that day. I helped her with a difficult patient and I passed out medication for all the patients on the floor, trying to get into her good graces, but to no avail.

The next day, she gave me a bad assignment. I had to take care of several difficult patients with no nurse's aide to help me. Other nurses commented on my assignment. One nurse said, "She's out to get you."

By Friday, I was frazzled and decided to confront "Nurse Ratchet," whose real name was Pat.

"Pat," I said, "is there something you don't like about me, or something I did? You seem to be angry and annoyed with me all the time."

She looked at me for a minute, checking me up and down and finally said, "Your heart isn't in this."

I was livid! I lost my temper. I screamed, "What do you mean by that statement? I love nursing!" She walked away from me without replying. I wanted desperately to run up to her, grab her thick Coke bottle glasses off her face and crunch them and scream, "So, how do you like that, four eyes?" Instead, I gave myself two minutes, walked up to her and said, "Pat, you're harassing me and if you do it again I'll report you to Administration!" She glared at me as I walked away.

That night, I started to rethink George's offer. I was getting spring fever, hating to go into work to face Pat and working the night shift. When George let me off for work at the front door of Mass General, I wanted to RUN! Escape! I felt claustrophobic as if I was going to suffocate — sickness, death, daytime insomnia; I needed Colorado!

I took care of a very spry elderly man that night who helped me with my decision to go to Colorado. He was about 80-years-old and had fallen down and broken his hip playing tennis. I said, "Mr. Ellery, you still play tennis?"

He replied, "Young lady, life is too short not to do everything you want to do. Life is about fun and risk taking." I knew the risk I would be taking if I left work and went out west, I could lose my job. I had been a nurse for just a year and a half and was on my second job already. That didn't look good on a resume.

The next day, I called George at work and told him I was going to Colorado. I said, "I don't want to lose my job; is there any way to get around this?" George showed up at dinner and told me he had a plan. He was going to call my head nurse Mary and tell her I was sick and needed to be out of work temporarily.

The next day, George called the floor and asked for Mary. When she got to the phone George said, "Mary, this is Dr. Feldman (fictitious name, of course) a patient of mine who is a nurse of yours, Kate Connors, is quite sick with mononucleosis and cannot be back to work for three to four weeks." I was snickering in the background and couldn't believe he was brave enough to do such a thing … and that it worked! Or so I thought. Mary called me that night to tell me she felt bad and to call her when I was ready to come back. She'd let the staff know. I knew "Nurse Ratchet" would have a field day with this piece of information.

I felt alive and free of worries for a while as we traveled west … six of us in the van having fun, lots of laughs and only $200 between us. The van broke down in Missouri and as I sat on a park bench by myself, waiting for the van to be ready, I started to feel guilty. My parents were livid at what I had done. I disappointed them once again. "You never think of the consequences, Katie," my dad said. I also felt bad that Mary was lied to. I liked her, and what I did was wrong. Not earth shatteringly wrong, but I felt guilty through most of the trip.

By July, we were back home and I moved back with my parents because Irene and her husband were separating. I ended up going back to work and getting stuck more on the night shift than before. I still had trouble sleeping during the day and I was irritable all the time. I tried to switch to another floor and didn't like what I was offered on the 3-11 shifts. I liked Orthopedics and the trauma end of nursing. *I will have to stick this out,* I thought.

Some of my friends were working 11-7. We would sometimes meet for coffee after work at someone's house. But the coffee turned into mimosas and lots of partying. "This is our night time," one of the nurses said. So, I went along with it, but I wasn't happy. A cloud was hanging over my head, an indescribable feeling of guilt and loneliness and always a feeling of impending doom. I ignored my feelings, worked, tried to sleep and partied through the next six months.

CHAPTER TWELVE

Downward Slide

It is hard to describe what happened to me in the next three years. I took a nosedive in my personal and professional life. I was a lost soul, crying for help but rejecting everyone. I called it my loss of spirit years.

I finally quit my job at Mass General and moved into an apartment in Belmont, a suburb of Boston, with my sister, Irene, and her son, Paul. I got a job working in a nursing home full time working the 3-11p.m. shift until I could decide what I really wanted to do.

This was my third job in two and a half years. I wasn't proud of myself for that. I had made some poor decisions. I had been doing too much partying, drinking and smoking pot. I gave in to drugs because George broke up with me. "Nothing personal, Kate," he said. "I just need my space." But I took it badly and my self-esteem and self-worth no longer existed. Nothing else seemed to matter except getting through work and going to Boston to party.

I was out of control several months later, and my family had to place me in a detoxification unit for three weeks. No one in my family could understand what was happening to me, nor could I. My spirit died and I didn't care if I lived anymore. In the detox, I became friendly with Janine, the registered nurse on the evening shift. She was the only one who could reach me. She was about ten years older than me and smelled like lilacs. I said one evening. "Janine, you smell great, like my mom's lilac bush in her backyard.

She said, "Tell me about your family, Kate."

So, I opened up to this very special nurse and bared my soul. "I have four sisters and I'm the only girl who screwed up," I said. I went on to tell Janine about my perfect sisters. Janet, who was thirteen years older than me, was living in New York, had two children and was a successful artist. "Kerry was my parent's favorite," I told Janine. "The one I was compared to my whole life." Then there was Renie, my soul-mate sister, and Denise, the youngest, most intelligent one. She was my parents' reward after dealing with me.

Janine said, "What are you going to do to help yourself when you get out of here? You can't go back to drugs, Katie. You'll die."

I didn't know and didn't care about what I was going to do. When I did get out, I went back to my parents' house, left the nursing home and got a job with an agency. I worked one day in a hospital, another in a nursing home or patient's house, wherever I was needed. But I ended up stealing drugs and getting caught and I had my nursing license suspended for two years. I was devastated! The only thing that gave me self-worth — being a nurse — was taken from me. But in retrospect, it had to happen. I think God reached down, put his powerful hands above me and said, "I need to help this poor child."

During those years, I found odd jobs — waitress, salesgirl, and finally working in a plant/flower store. I would spend my days making terrariums, filling the pots with different colors of sand, wondering where my life was going. I missed nursing and was frightened I'd never get my license back.

My dad had had major surgery and I went to visit him in the hospital. I knew the nurses in the recovery room, so my mother and I went in to see him right after his operation. As I pulled the blanket over my dad, my mom looked at me disappointedly and said, "You should be taking care of your father. When are you going to straighten out?"

I said, "Look Mom, I feel bad enough. Don't rub it in."

Years later, I asked my mother why she said that. "It hurts me, too. Why were you so cruel to me that day?"

"Oh, Kate, she said, "I was so afraid for you that I could only show anger. I wanted you to straighten out, be a nurse again."

I met my soon-to-be husband, Gary, right after that visit to my dad in the hospital. He put time and effort into our relationship and weathered my stormy days right along with me.

A year later, I got my nursing license back. Gary and I left Boston, drove to Colorado and settled in Denver with my girlfriend, Mary, from high school. Three weeks later, I received reciprocity and could work as an LPN in Colorado. I was nervous about going back to nursing and being around drugs, but never wanted to make the mistake of losing my license again because nursing was too precious to me.

I picked up a few shifts a week working for an agency. The fear of "screwing up" again left as I got back into the swing of taking care of patients in the hospital, nursing homes and clinics. I was on the mend. I had patients ranging in age from sixteen to eighty-eight. Many younger patients were transients who not from Denver — people much like myself, who came for a while and left. The year I was there, I never met one person who was originally from Denver.

After Gary and I were there for nine months, I found out I was pregnant. I knew I needed counseling and a decision needed to be made about my pregnancy. I went to a free women's clinic where I got emotional support. The counselors there helped me to decide to follow through with my pregnancy. The nurses at the clinic were a support service for the counselors; they ran educational classes for their clients regarding gynecological problems, birth control issues and communicable diseases. It was a fast, fascinating new world to me of the opportunities for nurses, the different fields they could get involved with in the medical profession.

As I took nutrition classes and learned about my baby's growth pattern, I said to myself, *I could do this and maybe I will. I could teach just like these nurses are teaching.* I was healing, getting well and promised myself there would be no more downward slides.

CHAPTER THIRTEEN

Courage to Change

In November of 1976, Gary and I moved to Seattle. My sister, Irene, was living there with her second husband, Artie. Gary and I wanted to be around family during my pregnancy, yet I didn't feel ready to go back East. Seattle was a magical city where I continued with my healing process. As my stomach blossomed, so did the smile on my face that I had been missing for over two years! My daughter would kick inside and keep me up all night with her activity, but I was so happy I didn't care. I was grateful to be alive.

My pregnancy brought me to one of the larger teaching hospitals for pre-natal care. I had to rely on free services because we had no medical insurance. My eyes were wide open to the way I was treated by the medical profession. I felt "less than" because of my economic status and the fact that I had been a drug abuser. I was low man on the totem poll.

The nurses would quickly take my blood pressure and leave, neither asking how I was doing emotionally nor mentioning my nutritional status. The doctors were ambivalent, unkind and indifferent; no one cared that I was putting on too much weight. I asked to see a dietician but to no avail.

During my pregnancy, I worked at a nursing home for young adults with kids who were physically and emotionally disabled by things such as muscular dystrophy, autism and brain damage. I gave those kids every ounce of energy I had emotionally and physically, but at the end of the shift, I felt I got nowhere. The first time I took care of an autistic child, he kept refusing to take his medication and would bang his head against the wall each time I approached him. The nurse on the previous shift said, "Tell him he won't have any dinner unless he takes his med."

Yikes! That didn't sit well with me at all! "Don't feed him?" I asked. That seemed to be the only happiness in his life. Later that evening, after refusing his medication one more time, I sat down next to him with a cup of pudding, I crushed his medication up, told him I put it in the pudding and said, "Please take this, Jerry." He looked so frightened and had marks on his forehead from banging his head against the wall, but he took the pudding and spoon, slurping it into his mouth. I felt I had accomplished something and he trusted me; I hated threatening patients.

I took care of a twenty-year-old muscular dystrophy patient as well. She was wheelchair bound, had uncontrollable muscular movement on all four limbs and couldn't prevent herself from drooling. But she had the best sense of humor! She would leave the home every day to take classes at the community college, and as she left she'd mumble (she was hard to understand) "I wonder how many books I'll drool on today and how many students I'll drool on. A great way to make friends. Right, Kate?" This was Julie's way of coping with her illness — laughter and jokes about her disease.

I said, "Julie, you keep me laughing like this and I'm going to sign you up for a comedy act on TV." And so it went on every day like that. But Julie worsened as the years went on. Her brilliant mind couldn't be challenged because the dystrophy was taking over and she had many complications. When she acquired a bad respiratory infection, depression took over. Her good attitude and jokes ceased. Julie was giving up, losing her will to live. I went on maternity leave, and I heard she died two weeks after the birth of my daughter.

After Jessie was born, we stayed in Seattle for almost another year. It was February of 1978 and we kept seeing pictures of the snowstorms of the 'blizzard of '78' back East on TV. I had my first feeling of homesickness. I was ready to go back home, show off my daughter to everyone and resume my life. The real Katie was back, I had the courage to change and I was ready to face the ghosts in the closet, or at least put them on the back burner. I wanted Jessie to grow up having a relationship with her grandparents. So, at the end of March, we packed our belongings into our white pick-up truck and headed east by way of Colorado to visit Mary one more time. Our new life was beginning.

CHAPTER FOURTEEN

Back to Boston

Twelve-foot snow banks lined the Massachusetts Turnpike as we entered the state. I cuddled Jessie next to me and said, "We're home, honey. Back to Boston."

We found an apartment in Belmont, a small town west of the city, where we continued to raise our daughter. I found a job on a Telemetry floor (cardiac) at St. Clemens Hospital in Cambridge, working the 3-11 shift three days a week.

Gary worked the day shift for the Public Works Department in Arlmont. He was with Jessie at night when I went to work, a routine we fell into easily. Jessie was the light of my life and my saving grace. Years later I heard my father say to Jessie, "Having you straightened your mother out." She was only five-years-old at the time and had no clue what her grandfather was talking about, but I understood and realized my dad was rooting for me all along.

Although I wasn't crazy about working on a Cardiac floor, I put my nose to the grindstone and made work a priority. I took a six-week course learning the functions of the heart and how to read heart monitors. There was a real camaraderie on the evening shift. Most of us had young children, could relate to each other's lives and support one another when we came into work exhausted after being up with a sick child all night.

My mother and father were thrilled that I was working in Cambridge, the place where they grew up. My mom would call me and say, "So, who did you take care of from Cambridge today? Anyone your dad and I would know?"

I'd say, "Mom, for the fifteenth time, I can't give out names. It's not professional. The patients don't want people to know they're sick either."

But she didn't get it! She'd say, "Katie, it's only me, your mother. I wouldn't say anything!" Then we'd laugh because we knew she'd tell my dad and it would be around Cambridge, that "so and so" had a heart attack.

One evening, my mother showed up on my floor equipped with camera to take a picture of me in my nurse's uniform, cap and all. I said, "Mama! You're embarrassing me and nurses don't wear caps anymore!"

She replied, "Come on, Kate. Stand right over there by that pretty window. I'll be quick." So, I reluctantly stood there as my patients peeked out their doors, laughing as my mother snapped away. "Now," she said, "I want a picture of the group of you."

"Mom," I whined, half angry, half serious, "this is a hospital; I'm at work not on an outing. Now GO," I said, as I quickly walked her to the elevator.

One thing I noticed in my profession since the day I started nursing school is that nurses get blamed for everything! If a patient's dinner tray wasn't delivered or if the linen wasn't picked up, it was the nurse's fault! The blame would go quickly to us and the nurse would have to make things right. Our role was very ever-expanding as well. Somehow, we could always be a nursing assistant, dietary aide, social worker, or even a maintenance man! I would often find myself climbing on a chair, trying to fix a light bulb or switch because the maintenance people were tied up. Clean floors? Of course, if something spilled and housekeeping wasn't around, we were there with the mop, making the floor shine.

The patients always seemed appreciative, no matter what. They, of course, were at our mercy and some patients could be very demanding and in need of attention. An elderly woman I took care of named Carmella was a "frequent flyer." A frequent flyer is a patient who is in and out of the hospital constantly. For instance, discharged on a Friday back in on Tuesday with the cycle repeating itself over and over. Some frequent flyers needed to be in the hospital, some didn't. Carmella was one who didn't, and cried wolf a lot.

One evening, we were extremely busy and we were short staffed. We were all running around trying to get our work done safely and efficiently. Carmella kept putting her call light on, needing attention. "Nursie, can I have more water? Can I have Jell-O? Or I need to go the bathroom." She craved attention and we tried to give it to her, but after the seventeenth time she put on her call light (yes we counted) we didn't run to her room anymore. When we didn't answer, she decided to find out for herself what the hold up was, but Carmella had to do it in style so we would really pay attention. I turned the corner of the hallway and there was Carmella, on all fours, crawling to the nurse's station. Her hospital gown wide open, her backside exposed and she yelled, "Help! Help! I've had a stroke!" It was hard not to laugh. I knew she was faking it. Two of us got Carmella in a wheelchair and placed her in front of the nurse's station for the rest of the shift where she remained happy, watching us all scurry around.

St. Clemens was a fun place to work. A small community hospital in Cambridge, Massachusetts, it serviced many people in the surrounding areas. It was a Catholic hospital and had a nun for an Administrator. She was nice but tough, very business oriented and hated the fact that the practical nurses organized a union during my employment there: She made life difficult and couldn't see our side of bringing in a union. Life was a battle after we unionized. The LPNs seemed to be bickering with administration about our job descriptions, hours and, of course, our wages. It was like pulling teeth to get validated and settle agreements. I tried not to let these disputes affect my general attitude and I realized how attached I was to this cozy little hospital.

The 3-11 shift from all the floors as well as the therapists would sit together, laugh, tell stories and joke around. I worked with a respiratory therapist named Jane. Jane was around 28-years-old and a comedian and practical joker. She'd do things such as fall down in the middle of the nurse's station and pretend she hurt herself. We'd all go rushing over to Jane saying, "What happened? You okay?"

And she'd say, "Ha … Ha … only kidding." She'd do little things like that daily, maybe weekly. We learned not to take her seriously. I remember a doctor saying to her in a stern voice, "One day something is really going to happen to you and no one will believe you!"

Well, two weeks later, several of us were sitting at a table in the cafeteria eating dinner when Jane grabbed her throat and started choking. Of course, we all thought she was faking as she was going "eeee," with throat sounds. Francine, the nurse's assistant said, "Jane, knock that shit off. We're trying to eat," as we continued to ignore her.

A visitor from the other table saw her distress, got up from his seat and performed the Heimlich maneuver on her! A big fat piece of roast beef came flying out of her mouth and we all stared in stunned silence. As Jane recovered from the ordeal, the visitor said, "What's wrong with you people? You're in the medical field and can't tell when someone's choking?"

Jane, now fully recovered, said, "Yeah, thanks guys. I could have died." I think Jane learned her lesson on being a "Wisenheimer" and a few of us learned our own lessons as well!

Sometimes after our shift, we'd go out for a drink at the Aku-Aku, a local Chinese restaurant. Over cocktails and spare ribs, stories would be told, some believable some not so believable. Meg, a fifty-year-old Irish nurse I worked with, told us a story that brought shivers to me for many days. Meg was very Irish, spoke with a brogue and could weave a tale like no one I knew. She was also very religious; spirituality was a big part of her life.

Meg described her patient, Mr. Leary, as a large framed seventy-year-old man who had his first heart attack at fifty. He went into cardiac arrest and was resuscitated successfully. Two years later, the same thing happened and his heart weakened. This heart damage was severe and he was constantly short of breath, had no energy and the quality of his life was dwindling. He had two more heart attacks after that and was resuscitated. Meg said he told the doctors to call it quits. "If this happens again, DON'T BRING ME BACK TO LIFE!!" But the physician refused. I told him he was only sixty-two-years-old and he would have to continue to revive him if he was his patient.

Meg took care of Mr. Leary in the cardiac care unit the following night. She said he was praying to God to just let him die, he didn't want to go on. "No more defibrillation machines, Meg. You tell them that," he said. Around 5 a.m., Meg heard Mr. Leary's heart monitor alarm. The CCU had individual rooms, all glassed in; the sliding glass doors were always left open. Meg ran to his room, the monitor had a straight line and Mr. Leary was blue.

"Call a code," she yelled to the secretary. Meg ran to Mr. Leary's room to start CPR but couldn't get in!

I said, "What do you mean you couldn't get in? You left the sliding door open!"

It was the force of our Almighty God that wouldn't let us in the room." She went on to say she tried to get in, but was pushed away by a wind-type feeling.

When the code team arrived, they saw her standing there and the doctor yelled, "Meg, why didn't you start CPR?"

"I can't get in the room," she hollered. The doctor charged past her and was immediately pushed back by the "force" as well. They stood there in stunned silence as Mr. Leary died before their very eyes. The chills ran up and down my spine as Meg told this tale with such belief and such conviction with her thick Irish brogue.

There was another similar story, one of my own and very real. I was on the code team, which consisted of nurses, doctors and the respiratory therapist. Each of us would have an assignment when the code was called stating the patient was in respiratory or cardiac arrest. At 10 p.m. on Friday night, the code 99 announcement came over the loud speaker. I ran down to the Emergency Room and it was Mr. Tocci, one of my all time favorite patients lying on the table. Carmen Tocci was a 49-year-old man with a family history of cardiac problems; his dad had died at the age of 38 from a heart attack and Carmen looked like he was following suit.

My job was to do compression. I had to stand on a stool and do them correctly, and each time I compressed his chest, I said, "Please, Carmen don't die, not tonight. Please, not this time." I looked over at my friend, Julie, as she was frantically getting medications ready to be administered to him … she loved Carmen as much as I did.

She said, "Come on, Carmen. I just got my diamond last night, I want you at my wedding." Ten minutes later, after 400 jolts (watts) of electricity from a defibrillating machine were administered, Carmen's monitor stopped straight-lining and he went into a normal heart pattern. "Phew!" we said, "Okay, Carmen. You rallied!" He was breathing but he was groggy and out of it. Ten minutes later, he was transferred to the cardiac care unit.

The next day, I went to visit him. He was wired up from the heart monitor, had an oxygen tube in his nose, intravenous in both arms with medications through the I.V. to keep his blood pressure stable and morphine for his chest pain. I said, "You made it."

He put his hand over mine and said, "I heard what you said, 'not tonight Carmen.'"

I was shocked! He was clearly dead at the point when I said those words. I replied, "You heard me? You knew I was there?"

"Yes," Carmen said. "You did compressions; I was watching you from the ceiling."

"The ceiling?" I said.

"Yes," replied Carmen, "I was floating, watching everyone and myself, deciding if I wanted to live. And by the way, tell Julie I want an invitation to her wedding."

On Memorial Day, I worked the day shift 7a.m. to 3p.m. As I was making a patient's bed, I looked outside onto Concord Ave. as a small parade was going by. In the midst of all the music, I heard sirens and saw the ambulance frantically trying to maneuver through the crowd of people to reach the Emergency Room!

It was a 22-year-old man who was injured. He was painting a house and had fallen off the ladder, about two stories, right onto a picket fence. About five minutes later, a jogger in his mid-fifties was running by the scene of the accident and he stopped and asked some observers, "What happened? I'm a doctor. I can help." Someone explained to him what had occurred and the jogger ran to the victim where a paramedic was treating him. The jogger/doctor looked down at the victim and looked into the face of his son.

For the next twenty-four hours, this man did not leave his son's side. He helped stabilize him, get him in the ambulance and took charge of his care. I heard the next day the young victim stabilized enough to transfer him that evening to a Boston hospital with his dad at his side. The whole hospital felt so sad, picturing the father jogging and stopping to help at the scene of an accident that turned out to be his son.

CHAPTER FIFTEEN

A Nurse with an Attitude

I found out in February of 1979 that I was pregnant with my son Dan. It was a good pregnancy. I was really taking care of myself; I jogged five days a week six miles a day until my eighth month and I continued working three evenings a week. Patients got nervous, fearful if I had to do anything strenuous for them. "Oh, no dear," they'd say, "I'll do it," or, "Go get another nurse, I don't want you lifting me up in my bed." This was okay with most nurses; they didn't mind helping, going overboard a little bit, but there were some nurses who were resentful and didn't feel as if a pregnancy was a good enough excuse to bow out of patients' care. Unfortunately, I had a supervisor who didn't cut much slack — pregnant or not.

It was two weeks before my due date; I was very pregnant and very tired. We were especially busy at work one evening. None of us went to supper and most didn't take a break. I told the charge nurse at 10 p.m. I needed to get something to drink. "No problem," she said. "Take your time." Unfortunately, I bumped into Margie, the evening supervisor, when I got off the elevator. Margie had two sides to her; she was either kind, compassionate and willing to help or a beast! Verbally abusive and critical, that night she was definitely the latter. As I exited the elevator she said, "Katie, what are you doing off the floor?"

I replied, "I went to get a Coke and took a break."

"A break!" she said, in astonishment. "Everyone else is running around crazy and YOU went for a break?"

I was fuming! Wanted to scream at her and say, "And where have you been, Margie, sitting in your office, feet up, not helping on the busy floors?" Instead, I took a deep breath and calmly said, "I worked it out with the heard nurse, Margie. It was only for a Coke and only ten minutes." She gave me a dirty look as I walked back to my floor. When she was out of sight, I turned, gave her the finger and mouthed to myself, "true asshole," and wondered how she could be so mean.

I worked up to two days before I delivered Dan. I went into labor on November 12, 1979, Veterans Day, a holiday in Massachusetts. My contractions started about 7a.m. I knew I was having a Caesarian section, so I woke Gary up and he called my physician at Newton-Wellesley hospital. My doctor was off that day but decided to come in for the delivery anyway.

Gary was extremely calm as we headed to the hospital. With Jessie, he had been nervous, jumpy; he was a totally different person. We were driving along and he pulled into McDonalds and I said, "What are you doing? Are you crazy?"

He calmly said, "I need a cup of coffee." I sat in the car fuming! I watched him walk out with a steaming cup of coffee (my most favorite thing in the world).

When he entered the car, I said, "Gary, you're an asshole. The one thing I'm craving and love more than anything, and you stop and get it for yourself! Besides, I'm having contractions."

"Oh, Katie," he replied, "we got time. You're overreacting."

"Easy for you to say, Mr. Chock Full of Nuts," I replied.

We arrived at the Emergency Room and a nurse brought me up to the delivery room area. Sarah, one of the delivery room nurses, started to prep me for surgery. She let Gary come into the room as she took my blood pressure, listened to Dan's heart rate and put a Foley catheter into my bladder. Gary sat there calmly reading the sports page — no, engrossed in the sports page — glancing over occasionally at me, smiling. I told Sarah I wanted to rip his throat out. She laughed and said, "Men are clueless. Aren't they?"

"Imagine if they had to have the baby!"

Two minutes later, we were in the delivery room. Gary was given a pair of scrubs to wear and he looked like one of the delivery team. My doctor was present, the anesthesiologist had just finished putting an epidural catheter in my spinal cavity for the section and Gary was holding my hand. I looked up at all three of them and realized these guys were in charge of my life and my newborn's life, and they were all under thirty! Yikes!

The delivery went well; they were professional and caring. I was nervous when they had my abdomen totally opened with contractors. Gary looked at me, I was helpless, paralyzed from the anesthesia, and through his mask he said, "Kate, your insides look like tripe." The doctors and nurses burst out laughing. Bruce Springsteen started to blare from a radio and two minutes later, the doctor yelled, "It's a boy!"

CHAPTER SIXTEEN

A New Personality Emerges

I stayed working at St. Clemens for a year after Dan was born, but I was getting restless and bored. I wasn't being challenged enough professionally. I felt as if I was stagnating, not being challenged. Gary and I had bought a house in Woburn, twenty minutes from the hospital, not really too far to drive, but when I got out at 11:30 at night I sometimes didn't want to make the trip because I was so exhausted.

One night, I got out of work an hour later because we had been very busy and I didn't finish up until 12:30 a.m. I walked to my car and put my pocketbook on the roof so I could scrape the ice off the windshield. After I finished, I was tired, spaced out and forgot I had put my purse on the roof of the car. Halfway home, I realized what I had done! Figuring my purse fell off along the way, I made a U-turn and headed back the way I came. As I turned the car around my pocketbook fell off the roof! I laughed myself silly all the way home, but realized it wouldn't have been funny if I had lost my pocketbook on route. I came to the conclusion that I was tired and not thinking, and it made me realize I wanted to be closer to home.

In the spring of 1981, I started to look for another job. I put in an application at a few community hospitals closer to home. Laureat Clinic Medical Center had been opened almost a year. I submitted an application and after two interviews, a tour, meeting other nurses and hearing positives about Laureat, I took the job and started working in September on a medical/surgical floor, the 3-11p.m. shift three days a week.

Laureat Clinic is a world-renowned health care facility that was established in 1926 by Dr. Frank Laureat. The clinic itself started up in Boston with its patients being hospitalized at different city hospitals if they needed an inpatient stay. They moved to their new site in November of 1980. It was laid out with a clinic on one side of the hospital and an inpatient 200-bed unit on the other side. I was assigned to 6 west, which a thirty-six-bed unit was shaped like a horseshoe. It was 90% surgical patients who after surgery, go to the recovery room for a few hours and when they were stabilized would go back to 6 west for the rest of their hospitalizations.

The first six months of work, I did a lot of observing and asked many questions. I was the only practical nurse amidst all registered nurses who were brilliant and helped me with my new role. At first, I felt inadequate and had to learn to accept constructive criticism, but as time went on I became confident and felt good about myself; a whole new personality emerged.

There were many nurses in my life who I looked up to, would ask for advice and who helped me develop more in my profession but one in particular will always remain someone who influenced my life positively in my beginning years at Laureat.

Her name was Irene Cooper. She was an intravenous nurse and an ace at her job. If no one else could get an I.V. line started, you knew Irene could. "Hot pack those arms, get those veins to pop," she'd say, as she limped away. Irene had some type of disability that affected her gait; other times I'd see her ambling along almost as if she couldn't go on, then suddenly, her beeper would go off and she'd pick up speed, almost running to the elevator. Whatever her disability was it didn't get her down; she never complained, never was lazy and always gave good advice and her opinion — whether you wanted to hear it or not.

"Confidence," she said to me. "If you have confidence, then anything can happen." And Irene was a confidence booster to me. Although she was curt, sometimes abrupt, she wouldn't leave unless she taught you correctly. And funny! A very dry, dry, sense of humor. The first bit of advice she gave me was, "Never trust anyone in this place that carries a clipboard. They are not trustworthy. They have another agenda and your welfare isn't on their agenda." I started noticing many of the "in charge" people carrying their clipboards after Irene had given me that piece of advice. "Snobs," she'd say, "really can't do much of anything except carry those clipboards with all those important papers!!" I laughed as Irene imitated these people as she carried the clipboard, nose up in the air with her unsteady gait, getting a kick out of herself.

What I liked most about my new job is that the patients got better. They had surgery and went home. Of course, there were those who were "open and close." These were people who came in for exploratory surgery because blood work, X-rays or other tests were not conclusive yet they still had symptoms of something being wrong. So, the surgeon would do surgery (open them up) but often times the patient was full of cancer so the surgeon would just close them back up and try for an alternative or palliative treatment such as chemotherapy. Often they were given only months to live, sometimes more with chemo, realistically they were just buying time.

These patients who were opened and closed were very difficult for me to deal with emotionally. I asked Bonnie, the charge nurse, "What do you say to the patient who left for surgery, hopeful and return to the floor groggy but able to say, 'How'd my surgery go?'" Bonnie said, "The doctor should be the one telling the patient, not us." And I realized the doctors did. But sometimes the patient was too medicated to remember and a few hours back on the floor, they'd expect an answer from us.

My consciousness on holistic medicine, which includes the healing of body, mind and spirit, started to change in the early 1980's. Although popular today, the healing of the body had nothing to do with the mind twenty years ago. But it did in my mind and other nurse's minds. I'd see a patient arrive at the hospital hopeful that their cancer would be removed and think positively. But after their surgery the surgeon would tell them it spread and needed more chemotherapy or radiation, the patient would often times give up, they'd lose hope and you'd hear of their death a few months later. Once they lost hope they physically could not heal on any level.

This was the case of Sam, a fifty-year-old man I took care of who presented himself with vague symptoms such as lethargy, lack of energy and weight loss. Sam entered the hospital with his family at his side saying, "If this is cancer I'm going to lick it." But Sam returned from surgery with a poor prognosis. The cancer was throughout his abdomen and in his liver. When he woke up, heard the words "spread" and "liver," he gave up. Two months later he was in the hospital dying, his skin jaundiced. He didn't even want to try chemotherapy to give him a few months. I took care of a similar patient years later named Emma, a woman in her sixties with a diagnosis of pancreatic cancer. She said to me, "They're not opening me up, I'm going to cure myself, and I'm not ready to die." She started on a course of dietary supplements, nutritional changes and mega vitamins. With her determination and will to live, she was not ready to leave this world. Her attitude and her mind took over and helped her heal. Five years later, I saw Emma in an aerobics class full of life and energy.

CHAPTER SEVENTEEN

No Choice

When my son Dan was six months old, I started taking courses towards my R.N./Associates Degree. I hadn't matriculated into any program but was easing myself back into the academic world. I started off taking an English/Writing course and got many of the liberal arts subjects out of the way before starting on the nursing courses.

During this period, in the early 1980s, the JCAH (joint commission of accreditation to hospitals) were redefining the role of the practical nurse. Functions I had been doing for years were being taken away. The LPNs gathered one day to talk with the Director of Nursing at Laureat about our concerns; we felt, as a group, these changes were very demeaning. Although the Director was sympathetic, understood our concerns, she felt her hands were tied. It wasn't a Laureat change but a JCAH change. "Go back to school," she said. "Get your RN." That was her advice. I felt I no longer had a choice, as if LPNs would be phased out of the medical profession in a few years.

Although I was seriously looking for the right nursing program to matriculate into, there was a patient I took care of on 6 west who made me rethink my decision about going back to nursing school.

His name was Leo. A forty-eight-year-old patient, who was relatively healthy, ran his own business and had a wonderful wife and two children. After a few tests, Leo found out he had stomach cancer. I met him on one of his inpatient stays at Laureat when he was first diagnosed. He had a positive attitude, was full of hope and couldn't imagine not getting better.

Leo was one of the finest men I'd ever met. A kind, caring gentleman, with a love of people in general and a family he valued. Leo was crushed the New Year's Eve he had to spend in the hospital. "I've never spent a New Year's Eve without my family," he said. "This is the first in years and years."

A few of the staff cheered Leo up that New Year's Eve. I told him he had the whitest teeth I've ever seen. "You were on one of the "Ipana" commercials when you were little," I said. We all laughed. But under that toughness there was a vulnerability and I could tell when I looked in his eyes he was getting discouraged. He was soon discharged and readmitted a week later with nausea, vomiting and dehydration. The chemotherapy was suppressing his bone marrow and his blood levels were off. I knew Leo was dying. "Why, God?" I said. "He is such a kind, giving human being. Why Leo?" I questioned life and its injustices and didn't see any fairness in life or for Leo and his family that they needed to watch him die. He was too good for that. The world needed more people like Leo.

Leo died a few weeks later with his family surrounding him. I watched his eighty-five-year-old mother walk out of his room in pain, suffering because her child was dying before her. "This isn't supposed to happen this way," she said. Leo's death hit me hard. I got too close to him and it was too painful. We were taught in nursing school not to get too close, but how do you control your feelings? How do you detach so easily and not get involved with patients and family when crisis hits?

I questioned my profession for a while after Leo died. Should I do something different in the medical field? Maybe look into ultrasound technician or an X-ray tech. But I knew that wasn't for me. I loved nursing, was passionate in my work. The following September I started nursing school; I was going to become a registered nurse.

CHAPTER EIGHTEEN

Another Episode

I was thirty-one years old. What was I doing back in school full time with two kids, a husband and a part time job? Gary was exhausted three months into my schooling; he had extra responsibility for the kids after he got out of work and he wasn't handling the situation well. My mother-in-law confronted me, told me I should wait to go back to school when Jess and Dan were older plus she was worried about her son, her "baby" her thirty-one-year-old baby taking on too much. I rolled my eyes and mumbled, "Typical Italian mother."

In looking back, she had a valid point. I left my kids with too many babysitters, one of them, a family member who caused emotional damage to my children that was not noticeable to me at the time. But I was on a mission, nothing would stop me from getting my RN and if Gary didn't want to stay with me, he didn't have to. But of course, he did because there was light at the end of the tunnel and it was the right thing to do.

Sutton Hospital, where I attended nursing school, is a small community hospital-servicing clients from surrounding towns. Not like a big city hospital yet similar in some ways because of it being closer to Boston; it had its share of emergencies such as gun shot wounds, drug overdoses and occasional gang related incidents. The Emergency Room always seemed to be hopping any time of the day or night.

The school was adjacent to the hospital where academics were held three days a week and clinical two days at the hospital. My days started at 5:30 a.m. and ended at midnight. I'd run from school to work at Laureat and fall into bed exhausted at 12 p.m. only to get up at 5:30 the next day and start all over again. There was such a contrast between the two facilities. Laureat, a world renowned teaching hospital where affluence was noted, to Sutton, a blue collar city and facility where poverty abounded, yet it had a wonderful community atmosphere, took care of its own and never refused health care.

I helped run a smoking cessation program at Sutton for six-weeks. One of my patients who had bladder cancer was in the group. He was only 55 years old and knew he had to quit smoking but was struggling. "It's such an addiction," he said. But he came faithfully to all the meetings and realized he depended on cigarettes as his "friend". He said, "Stopping this habit is like a death, but if I don't stop I'll die."

I'd go to work 3-11:30 p.m. at Laureat after being at school all day, hoping for a quiet night at work. But there never was a quiet night or empty bed. If a patient was discharged, two minutes later the Admission Office would call with another admission. By the end of the night, I'd want to pull my hair out! No more admissions, God. Please! But they came in droves and none of us ever stopped. When we'd go to dinner, my head nurse, Bonnie, would say, "I don't want to discuss illnesses, patients or cancer or I won't sit here!!" We would all laugh for forty-five minutes and talk about anything but work, knowing we had the rest of the night ahead full of dressing changes, monitoring vital signs and much more.

When a nurse went to dinner, she had to find another nurse to cover her patients. One evening, I was covering Melissa's patients. Melissa was a new graduate and had only been a nurse for six months. Melissa and I made rounds together on her patients so she could tell me about them and any issues. We went into Room 621. "Mr. Roland needs pain medicine at 6:00 p.m.," she said, then in 622, "Mrs. Avery needs her dressing changed at 6:30." In Room 623 Melissa said, "Mrs. Burger's I.V. is positional."

I looked down at Mrs. Burger; her 90-year-old eyes were shut, mouth agape and she was stone cold! I said, "Melissa, Mrs. Burger is dead. Do we need to code her?"

Melissa, in shock, shook her head no. "The family wants no heroics. God," Melissa said, "she was alive ten minutes ago!" This was Melissa's first death and she was slightly overcome by it all.

"Go to dinner," I said, "I'll call the doctor." At the end of the night, we all started to laugh about the incident and how we found Mrs. Burger. Although we were sad that someone we all knew had died, she was better off as she was ninety years old and full of cancer. "IV not dripping," I said jokingly to Melissa.

"Yeah, death will make an IV positional," said Leah.

Melissa cracked a smile and said, "What a dork I am! Mrs. Burger was stone cold and I'm trying to get her IV going."

The next morning at Sutton, I took care of a 25-year-old woman who had an ectopic pregnancy, two little kids at home, no husband and no insurance. "I got to get out of here," she told me. "I can't afford to be in the hospital."

That night at Laureat I took care of a very wealthy 75-year-old Arab. His family bought a house in Arlmont while their father was having chemotherapy for six-weeks. When I walked into the patient's room, he was sitting on the sink chanting and praying. "Please," I said, "get off the sink. You'll fall." Although there was a communication problem, he understood and I walked him to the chair while I made his bed. When I grabbed the bottom sheet $900 fell out! Hundred dollar bills trickled to the floor! When his son came in later that evening, I said, "I found this money. He had it under the mattress."

"Pfhh," his son said. A "pfhh" like "oh, well, it's only money." I thought of my 25-year-old patient that day, no insurance, no money and what she could have done with $900!

CHAPTER NINETEEN

Laughter: The Best Medicine

I had the pleasure of working with Bonnie, the charge nurse on the 3-11 shift for three years. Bonnie possessed one of the most important qualities to have, especially in the medical field — a sense of humor. She kept me laughing for three years; we would look at each other and burst out laughing. She was quick witted, didn't mind talking back to the doctors and always had a joke to tell.

One evening Bonnie was looking up laboratory results in the computer on a patient; she was sitting on a rolling chair and she stood up from the chair to answer a patient's call light and when she went back to sit down a doctor had come by, moved her chair and Bonnie fell right on her butt! What a sight! She was laughing so hard we had to help her off the floor, but Bonnie's laugh was so contagious we kept laughing. As we tried to pull her up, we'd go into stitches and she'd fall back again!

The next week, (still occupying the same chair and same computer) she realized she dropped her pen under the desk. Bonnie got down on all fours under the computer to retrieve her pen. In the meantime, Dr. Broswell, one of the surgeons who was 6'10", asked Bonnie to get a lab result. Still on her knees, she went to the computer, punched in the results and said, "Here you go, Dr. Broswell." Not knowing he was right next to her, she turned to tell him again and as her head turned, her face was right on the same level with Dr. Boswell's crotch! Her face turned beet red and, still on her knees, she looked up the length of his body and said, "Oh, hi."

Several of us were giggling. Lucille, one of the staff nurses, was laughing so hard she was wetting her pants and had to go to the bathroom! Bonnie recovered, got back on her chair and pretended like nothing happened until Dr. Broswell left the nurses station. Then she yelled, "I'm so embarrassed! How am I going to face him again!?"

I laid into her, "Yeah, Bonnie. I mean really: 'Oh, hi,' as you're face to face with crotchville?"

Then there was Grace. Grace was a patient who was in and out of the hospital all the time, and she was a whiner. Bonnie was at the desk doing paperwork and answering the patients' call lights and Grace put her light on every ten minutes for different silly reasons. She just really needed attention. At 10 p.m., after calling the nurse's station for the umpteenth millionth time, Bonnie's fuse was short and through gritted teeth she said, "What now, Grace?"

She replied, "I need my dentures cleaned."

At her wit's end, Bonnie said, "Look, Grace, if you took care of your teeth when you were younger you wouldn't need dentures." There was silence from Grace the rest of the shift. Bonnie said, "What's the matter with me? I can't believe I said that!"

A patient walking by the nurse's station said, "Grace is a pain in the ass. She's been bothering me the whole night, the old hag!"

***

My classes and clinical in school were not too difficult. It was an accelerated program of two years with only a few weeks off. We had to attend classes' right through the summer.

I had one instructor named "Ste-phaan," and you had to make sure you pronounced his name correctly. Anyway, Ste-phann was about thirty-five-years-old, tall, with bleached blond hair, full of life and hysterical! He was also very out of the closet and let it be known he was gay and was in a relationship, a serious one. He kept us all laughing with his quick wit and realistic view of life.

Some days, working on the medical floors with him, I would laugh so hard I'd have to hold my stomach. His mannerisms and voice launched me into gales of laughter! One day, after one of his better jokes, I cracked up and backed into a pool of urine from a patient who had wet the floor. I proceeded to lose my balance and fell in the urine. My cap fell off my head and I sat there, in astonishment, as some bigwig doctors walked past me, looking strangely as I sat there in the pee. Ste-phaan said, "Oh, doctor, these students …," in his most feminine voice.

Ste-phaan had an angry side that I witnessed one day when I was late for clinical. I had to work with him observing me in charge of the floor on the 3-11 shifts for a full week. Well, the first day, I was late. I had trouble finding a babysitter and literally ran onto the floor, shoelaces untied and cap in my hand instead of on my head. Ste-phaan said, "Katie, you're a slob and you're a late slob. Get over here and get your assignment!"

I was pissed! He was only a few years older than me. Why was he belittling me? My intuition told me something was wrong. Although I was angry, halfway through the shift I said, "Steph, what's up? Why did you flip out on me?"

He said (in his most feminine voice), "Oh Kate, I'm sorry. I had a fight with Felix (his significant other) and I haven't been myself since we've quarreled."

"That's okay," I said, "happens in every relationship." But the whole time he was telling me this story, I couldn't wait to tell Gary! My husband, Mr. Macho, loved hearing Ste-phaan stories. A year later, on graduation night, my husband went over to him, shook his hand and said, "I've finally met Ste-phaan."

Two days before Valentine's Day, all the students were discussing what we would buy our boyfriends/husbands for Valentines Day. Ste-phaan (loving this subject) said, "Girls, girls, girls. There is only one thing you can do for your hubbies — dye your pubic hair blonde and manicure it into the shape of a heart. I'm telling you they'll love it."

Thirty years later, I say thank you to Ste-phaan for his wit, his intelligence and his ability to keep us laughing when we wanted to quit. Without him, I would not have made it through school. Laughter is the best medicine.

CHAPTER TWENTY

Oh No, Not the Emergency Room

In school, we had to do a couple of weeks in the Emergency Room, which wasn't my cup of tea. At Laureat I worked in the ER when they were short staffed and I hated going there. I didn't like the fast pace or the routine; so, when I had to do a week of nights I dreaded it. But fears can be worse than actual fact. I enjoyed myself, and in the process, I learned quite a bit.

Beverly was the nurse I had to follow, report to. She showed me what to do and how to do it. Bev was a middle-aged woman with a buxom body, flaming teased red hair and "knew her shit" as one doctor told me. She had been an ER nurse for many years, "zillions" of years as she put it. But most of all she loved the night shift and thrived on traumas. "It's the adrenaline rush," she'd say. I became close to Bev. For some reason our personalities clicked, even though I told her I hated the ER and the night shift. I told her my horror stories of working the night shift and how I took a rectal temperature on a resident. I had her in stitches laughing; she was crossing her legs so she wouldn't pee her pants! (Is this a trait of all nurses?) We laughed as I told her tales and she related stories to me. Bev was open minded, knowledgeable and a good person to bounce stories off of. I told her how I pretended I had mononucleosis and had my boyfriend call my supervisor at Mass. General so I could go to Colorado. Beverly said, "God, Kate, what balls! What imagination!"

I looked at her in astonishment and said, "You mean you don't think that was a screwed up thing to do?"

Bev said, "No, you both were very inventive. Give yourself a break; you were only 21-years-old!"

"Geeze," I said, "I've beating myself up emotionally all these years and you say I was a creative thinker."

Bev was used to the older generation, the Geritol group, coming in for treatment in the ER. She told me they were better known as Gomers. "Gomers?" I said.

"Yes," Bev replied, "means Get Out of My Emergency Room."

These were patients who appeared on Friday night at 11:20 when your shift was ending. They were confused people with no control over their urinary or gastrointestinal systems (shit everywhere) and oftentimes they were also combative. In other words, everyone's worst nightmare, not exclusive to the ER. When these gray/blue heads appeared in the ambulance, it was time for concern. A Gomer was arriving, being admitted with a vague diagnosis (actually, the family may have needed a break and wanted them admitted!) such as FTT (failure to thrive), dehydration or congestive heart failure. So these poor souls would look at you with their sad, lonely eyes saying, "Please, help me."

Bev was great with the cardiac arrests. I observed her doing a precordial thump (which is a hard thump on the chest with your fist) as the person went into a full code. The EKG would straight line but after a thump, air and compressions, a life would be brought back. Bev was an ace at codes. After a forty-five-year-old man came in with a full blown cardiac arrest, I witnessed Bev bring him back to life and back to his family; another Carmen at St. Clemens's.

One night when I first arrived in the ER, the place was hopping. The phone was ringing off the hook and I caught it on the eighth ring. "ER, Katie speaking," I said. It was a teenage girl, fourteen years old, who thought she was pregnant.

I asked her if she had missed a period. "Yes," she responded. She sounded young, scared and unsure, so I proceeded. "Have you missed two periods?"

"Oh, yes!" she replied.

"When, exactly, was your last period?"

Total silence for a minute then she said, "Christmas." That meant she was over four months pregnant! She started to cry saying, "I don't want a baby." I asked if she could tell one of her parents. "Oh, no! I'll get thrown out of my house."

I said, "Look, you need to take care of this. Tell someone, please. Come into the Emergency Room. It is safe here and we'll help you!"

Beverly had appeared and looked at me with the expression, 'you need help?' I wrote on a piece of paper: Pregnant, fourteen! She mouthed the words, "try to get her in here." But this young girl couldn't bring herself to make a commitment.

She had told me she was a freshman in high school, so I said, "Is there a teacher you can tell or a counselor at school?"

"Yeah, Mrs. Christianson, my English teacher."

I said, "Please, come in tonight, if not go to her in the morning." Well, this poor girl never showed up nor did we hear from her again. I pictured her denying the pregnancy and delivering the baby in the bathroom at a high school dance.

I received a similar phone call two nights later. It was Mandy. She was sixteen and thought she was pregnant. So, I went through the same questions as before, "missed periods?"

"Well, no," she said.

"What makes you think you're pregnant?" I asked.

"Well," Mandy replied, "Tony, my boyfriend, well we were both naked and his penis was near my vagina but it didn't go in."

I was picturing this scene as she was describing it. *Ugh!* I thought. "Well, Mandy, did any sperm maybe seep in?"

"Oh, no," she said, "his thing was just lying there."

I said, "Mandy, you're not pregnant and I think you need to rethink about Tony; you're too young."

"But he loves me and says he loves me 'sooo' much he wants to have sex."

"How old is Tony?" I asked.

"Oh, maybe thirty," Mandy replied.

"Get rid of Tony. He only wants sex." I visualized sleazy Tony, manipulating and romancing — probably bought her a cheap yellow rose on some street corner! "Please, Mandy, break up with him."

CHAPTER TWENTY-ONE

Forty Days and Forty Nights

During the summer of 1984, the students had to do a psychiatric rotation for six-weeks at Metropolitan State Hospital. For a normal person, one who didn't grow up in a dysfunctional home, the six-weeks would have been a piece of cake. But I, Katie Connors Genovese, had to face all the ghosts of years past for the next forty days.

When I was younger, probably in third grade, my mom would take me and my brothers and sisters for rides through Metropolitan State Hospital and McLean Hospital, another local psychiatric facility. She'd cram all seven children into her large 1955 Chevy station wagon and off we'd go. The only one not present was my dad.

Why didn't he go? Well, my dad was the real reason we were going on this joy ride from hell. My father was drinking again, and although our family didn't suffer the daily active drinking, he had binges. Months would go by before he picked up again, but when he did, none of us could stand it, especially my mom. We'd venture out in the early evening to see "the crazy people" as my mother put it. I knew she meant no harm as I looked back on those episodes. My mother was trying to escape the effects of alcoholism and protect us in her own way. She was avoiding the craziness in our home, probably figuring these people were worse off than us. Our family and my dad didn't seem so crazy after seeing the patients in these mental institutions.

But I was a frightened kid, and as we would enter the hospital grounds and the old station wagon ascended the long winding roads, I'd be aware of every bump and rattle of the car and then I'd spot the "crazy" people. These patients would only be walking around, causing no harm and a car full of kids (maybe crazy people) would stare at them as we passed by. My two brothers picked up on my anxiety and tried to push me out of the car. My mom would drive slowly, wanting the time to pass, hoping my dad would be asleep when we returned. Those rides were long — never-ending in my eight-year-old mind — and always impacted my life negatively. I was deathly afraid of "going crazy" and being "locked up".

Twenty-five-years later, I was making this same trip by myself in my maroon Ford Escort, driving the long, winding road to my first clinical experience at Metropolitan State Hospital. As my anxiety appeared, I'd chant to myself, "Kate, you can do this," and I did do it. For forty days and nights, I lived my nightmares. The courage and strength came from somewhere.

I took care of the mentally ill who heard voices, were psychotic, depressed and suicidal. They were young and old, poor and even indigent. Most wore heavy clothing and dressed as if it were winter in 90 degree weather because the medications they were on affected the thalamus gland, which is a body temperature regulator. They didn't know the difference.

I was scared at times and couldn't eat or sleep; I lost five pounds. After two weeks, I knew I had to have closure of my past. I went to my nursing instructor and told her my tale of the scared eight-year-old kid creeping up the hill in the old Ford station wagon twenty years ago. Mary Ann, my instructor, listened intently. Replying, she said, "Kate, you're okay. You're a good student, a mother and wife; you're psychologically sane! Your mom should never have done that; she violated you, your siblings *and* the patients!"

From that point on, I felt better, validated. I wasn't crazy after all. I was just brought up crazy and dysfunctional because of the affects of living with an alcoholic. I started looking at my patients as humans who had love and fears, just like me. The Bills, the Lisas and the Johns, all with a painful past just like me. These patients all had something in common — trauma in their formative years, including abuse, physical and sexual; neglect by parents or the death of a parent.

Lisa, one of my patients, was 28-years-old diagnosed with schizophrenia. When she was five, her parents left for the evening and she had to baby-sit her three-year-old sister, Meg. Well, Meg fell out of the second story bathroom window and died. Lisa blamed herself and was never the same. She started hearing voices at age eight that told her she was a bad girl. She had been institutionalized most of her life.

Another patient, who called herself "Eve," had been physically and sexually abused by her stepfather most of her life. Eve hated her mother because she never protected her. Eve also had a fascination for Elvis Presley. She loved him and he loved her, she told me one day.

Four years before, Eve went home to the house she was sharing with her mother and thought her mother was sleeping with Elvis, so she burned the house down. Eve had been hospitalized since that time. She would frequently lose her temper, become combative and act inappropriately. One morning, while eating breakfast, Eve pulled down her pants in the cafeteria and started defecating. No discharge was in the near future for her.

Then there was Billy, a gorgeous 25-year-old with a sexual disorder. He was in and out of the hospital all the time. He couldn't control his urges. During a hospitalization, he would improve because of medication, administration and therapy. But as soon as he was discharged, he would go off his drugs. "I hate the side effects," he told me. But he was dangerous sexually and needed to be kept away from society.

I read his medical history one day. It stated his father sexually abused him but the worst part was the father made him watch as he sexually abused his sister. Billy was only two when this started happening and it went on for many years.

During this clinical rotation, I met a really cool thirty-five-year-old nurse named Ginger. She was only 4'11" and weighed 190 pounds. She was blessed with a wonderful attitude and was always singing and laughing with the patients. She never lost it emotionally … she loved her job. At the end of my rotation, when I was at my wit's end, I said, "Ginger, I admire you. How do you stand all this insanity day in and day out and maintain such a good attitude?"

"Sex," she replied, "whenever and as often as I can. It keeps me sane and helps me cope."

I was taken aback by her frankness and honesty. Gary and I laughed about it when I told him the story.

"Is she married?" my husband joked.

"Pretty sure," I replied.

"Lucky guy!" Gary said.

Later that evening, my husband was reading the paper and he yelled to me in the other room, "Hey, Kate, they're looking for RNs to work at Met State. Why don't you apply?"

Metropolitan State Hospital was in a beautiful area in Waltham, Massachusetts. It sat on several acres of land with lush green grass and manicured trees surrounding the buildings. Thirty years ago, it housed 1,900 patients and in 1984, the hospital only had 400. This was due to the deinstitutionalization of patients, which began in the 1950s. It became popular in Massachusetts in the late '70s, with politicians being advocated to get mental patients out of hospitals and mainstreamed with the rest of society, but having day programs available.

At the Pine Street Inn, a major shelter for homeless people, the staff was discovering a large number of men and women showing up each afternoon in search of a bed. These people were former mental patients who had been deinstitutionalized, regressed in the community, and were no longer able to function in society. The reaction was that of outrage and it forced Mental Health Commissioner Robert Okin to open the Parker Street Shelter.

Advocates for deinstitutionalizing stated the walls were crumbling at Met State, the heating system was deteriorating and patients were huddled together in dilapidated wards and day rooms. This led to more of a consolidation of the seven state mental facilities. The patients were slowly being pushed to the streets full of fear, anxiety and violence.

The last day of class, I patted myself on the back and said, "You made it, Kate. You got your ghosts out of the closet and actually managed to help a few people."

Ten years later, the buildings are empty, deserted but the lawns and shrubs remain manicured. Even popular motion pictures are filmed on the grounds of Metropolitan State Hospital. But where have the patients gone and has deinstitutionalization been working? Many politicians say yes, the mentally ill are living in group homes and mainstreaming with society. They are being set up in day programs and work, making them feel useful and part of society. The ones against this theory feel the mentally ill were thrown out of their safe nests where they were comfortable and that they didn't adjust well to the change. Many regressed and didn't stay on their medications.

Whatever the answer may be, it is up to the department of mental health, our politicians and those in favor of deinstitutionalization to provide mental health services to these people and comply with the *Americans with Disabilities Act of 1990*. Although there is constant restructuring within the mental health system, it needs to ensure a responsive and appropriate system of care focusing on our most vulnerable citizens.

CHAPTER TWENTY-TWO

Light at the End of the Tunnel

I had another year to go before I finished school. I was tired, Gary was tired and my kids never saw me and begged me to quit. They were sick of babysitters and not having their mom at home. Plus, we were broke. I hadn't been able to pick up any extra shifts and we were living paycheck to paycheck. No extra cash.

I told Gary I'd take a year off from school, we'd regroup, and I'd work more and go back to school the following year. But we both knew that would never happen. Money would start coming in and that would be it, I'd never go back. Gary said, "Continue and get it over with, there's light at the end of the tunnel." Another year of torture, and then we'd be on easy street financially. RNs made quite a bit more money than LPNs.

I would occasionally pick up a private duty case when they arose. "Speculating," or private duty, was easy work. The nurse was on-on-one with a patient and the money was good. The family paid privately.

I took a private duty case, a 60-year-old gentleman from New York, needing bowel surgery. For a week, I picked up extra shifts, cared for his IV, changed his dressings, and monitored his vital signs. His name was Bob and he had gold jewelry dripping from his body, and money and status written all over his face. He was very sure of himself, had a big ego and bragged about his ever-growing car dealership. It was an easy, uncomplicated case; when he slept, I studied.

On the last night caring for him, he was feeling better physically, was very talkative and ended up propositioning me! He stated he wanted a mistress, someone from out of town who he would put up in a fancy hotel once a month and he would pay me. "Are you interested?" he asked.

I have to say I was shocked. I had never met anyone so blatant and honest about his intentions. I quietly and simply declined the offer. When I walked out of the room and went to the nurse's station, I said, "Yuck!" to Phil, our secretary. "Phil," I said, "Mr. Bob wants me to go to New York and sleep with him once a month! He's my father's age, he's close to being bald and drags his one piece of white hair over his head to make it look like he has hair."

Phil laughed and said, "Kate, are you crazy? Reconsider. He'll pay you money that you need! Just get real shit-faced and you won't even know it's him."

"Yuck again," I said. "I'd know the next day that I was with him. No way; can't do it."

Mr. Bob was discharged two days later. Hopefully he went home alone, with no nurse accompanying him. Three years later, while visiting my sister in New York, I saw Mr. Bob on TV promoting his car dealership. He looked unchanged and sleazy as ever. No thanks, Bob!

***

In school, I had a rotation at Cambridge City Hospital on a medical floor. This was my father's old stomping grounds. He had been on the City Council in Cambridge and the Board of Trustees for the hospital. When I told my dad I would be there for three months, he started to beam! Every day he'd call me to see if I'd met anyone he knew. I'd laugh and say, "Dad! Remember from before, patient confidentiality?" But I shared stories of the hospital with my father, the politics going on and the ever-growing needs of a city hospital.

Cambridge City cared for a diverse group of people, from the homeless to the affluent and well educated, not catering to one particular group just caring for the wealthy and the indigent. But the number of homeless is what struck me. They would arrive in the ER, drunk, dirty and sometimes confused with the beginning of the DTs. Some were hungry and dehydrated and had nowhere to go.

I took care of my first patient who had scabies, a skin disease caused by the transmission of crab-shaped mites that causes irritation with increased itchiness and rash. This can be spread easily amongst the homeless. It was so sad watching them arrive. You'd look at them and wonder what their medical needs were, when you thought all they needed was a good shower and a change of clothes.

Homelessness was becoming an ever-increasing social problem in the 1980s in all the major cities in the United States as well as smaller communities. The causes ranged from large-scale deinstitutionalization of mentally ill people to the disintegrating affects of society itself, drug and alcohol abuse, job loss and cutbacks in federal social welfare programs during the Reagan administration.

In Boston, there were not enough homeless shelters. Most of the homeless were men, although good percentages were women and children. I walked into a thirty-year-old man's room one day. He was homeless and had been admitted the day before for pneumonia. I knew him. He was the son of a politician my dad knew, and we had been introduced at a fund-raiser five years before.

We locked eyes, but he didn't acknowledge that he knew me nor did I show any recognition. I thought he'd be embarrassed because he was so disheveled. He had been so inebriated the night before and showed the effects that day. His hair was dirty and he needed a shave badly. His shoes had no laces and there were holes in the toe areas.

A male orderly gave him a shower and cleaned him up. By the end of the week, his pneumonia had resolved and he was sober and very handsome. But the sadness remained in his eyes. When he was discharged, I wondered where he would go. Did his dad or mom know his whereabouts? Was he estranged from his political family because of his alcoholism and homelessness?

I had another female patient at Cambridge City who was fifty years old and had multiple sclerosis, which is a neurological disease that causes a breakdown of the myelin sheath, (which covers the nerves). This causes mild to severe changes to the nervous system. My patient, Marie, had the worst-case scenario and was wheelchair bound, but was able to stay at home and maintain some independence with the help of home health aides.

She had an exacerbation of her illness and needed short-term hospitalization to regulate her medication. Unfortunately, Reaganomics were in full swing and many of the Federal cutbacks were aimed at Medicaid and the disabled. Marie found out two days before her discharge that her services were being discontinued at home. "Why?" she asked. "I want to live independently for as long as I can, but I need the aides to help me every day. How am I not going to end up in a nursing home?"

I felt badly about Marie and her situation, so on my way home from school I stopped by my dad's office in Waverly. Since his retirement from the telephone company, he worked in Tip O'Neil's congressional office as an aide. I told my father about Marie, her cutbacks and her illness.

"Is there anything you can do, Dad? Pull some string politically?" I asked.

He took down all the information he needed and a week later, all of Marie's previous services were reinstated, restoring my belief that all politics are local.

After Christmas break, we had our last rotation at Melchester Hospital, a small wealthy hospital in Melchester, Mass. with over two hundred beds. At this facility, we were going to do our clinical in pediatrics and obstetrics. I thought it would be a breeze. I was wrong. My last rotation was my hardest. I never realized how many illnesses there were in infants and children — heart problems at birth, babies born drug addicted with complications and needing detoxification, etc.. It was an eye opener. I was thrilled at the learning experience and exhausted from all the running around. My emotions were all over the place. When I had to face and take care of a seven-year-old boy who needed a tonsillectomy, it was beginning to become overwhelming.

Tom presented himself to the Melchester Emergency Room (accompanied by a hysterical mother) with a temperature of 101, sore throat and chills. The doctor decided to keep him overnight and observe. The next morning, I had to obtain a throat culture. I had to convince Tommy to let me stick a long Q-tip down his throat.

"You'll gag a little but it will be over fast," I said.

"No!" he screamed and sat there with his mouth clenched tight! He wouldn't budge.

I was nice at first. "Tommy, please let me do this. If I don't get it, my teacher will be mad at me!" I said.

"Who cares," Tommy replied.

I tried the firm approach. "Tom, open your mouth this minute." Still he wouldn't budge. Finally, angry, I reached into my pocket and pulled out a dollar bill. I said, "Okay, Tommy, we're at this point. I'll give you this money if you just open your mouth and stick out your tongue!"

"Two bucks," he said.

I angrily handed him the two dollars, obtained the specimen and walked away laughing and thinking how bad I was with kids!

In the middle of March, I found out I was pregnant again. Gary was outside our house chopping wood when I told him. He looked up at me in disbelief. "How?" he said.

"Gee, I wonder," I replied sarcastically. He shook his head and started to smile.

My son, Dan, who was five said, "Really, Mom? A dog would have been fine. You didn't have to go to all that trouble."

Two weeks later, I started to throw up every morning. Joyce, my instructor for Obstetrics, was getting annoyed at me leaving class each day. After class one day, I told her the circumstances. "I'm leaving class each day because of morning sickness," I said.

She didn't respond and didn't seem to care, just continued with her task at hand. It was then that I realized she just didn't like me. On a daily basis, she was making my life miserable. I was hormonally fragile and her disdain toward me just made it worse. She criticized me, tried to belittle me and I would fight off the tears. As she would chastise, I would be fuming, wanting to yell, "I know what I'm doing! I'm a mother with kids." Instead, I'd remain quiet and not stick up for myself.

I drove to my parents' house one day after clinical. It was early spring and my dad was outside puttering in his garden, planning his planting season. He looked up and knew something was wrong. "What's up, Katie?" he asked.

We sat on the picnic table as I described the last few weeks with my instructor. "I can't take it anymore, Dad. I'm going to quit school. I can't stand the harassment."

My dad replied, "So your gonna let the old battle-ax get the better of you? That's what she wants ... you quitting. That means she won. She had power over you! Look, Kate," he went on to say, "there are going to be a million Joyces in your life. Rise above it, even stand up for yourself. You only have a couple of months to go!"

I left that day knowing I was not a quitter. I had to suck it up, gather strength and not take abuse from the "battle-ax."

Towards the end of May, we had one instructor named Patty, who gave a lecture and offered suggestions to us on joining our Nurses Association and events that could keep us involved in the politics of nursing in Massachusetts.

"Nurses are the biggest group of women in the world, collectively, and if we stick together, bond and nurture on one another's positions, women/nurses can only blossom."

She went on to say how we would be faced with ethical and legal dilemmas and we must be aware of exceeding the legal parameters in our profession. In other words, we would constantly be faced with moral and ethical issues.

"Biggest group of women in the world collectively." I repeated what she had said, and thought, *We are our own worst enemies because we don't stick together enough.* Over the years, in all the different health care facilities I had worked in, the biggest problem to me was gossip. Instead of trying to work out problems and issues that arose, nurses would talk behind one another's backs. Oh, not everyone, but there was always one who would gossip and be the instigator, trying to make trouble. Nurses, in my opinion, needed to work on effective communication skills, work together and solve problems together, not apart.

I told Patty how much I enjoyed her lecture and how I felt about nursing in general. "What made you want to become a nurse?" she asked. I went on to tell her about my younger sister, Denise, and the hospitalization when she was 13, her scoliosis and bed rest for nine months and how I fell in love with the whole idea of being a nurse. Helping, nurturing the sick, I wanted to help people get better.

I told Patty about Lisa, a four-year-old who was in the same hospital as Denise twenty years before. Lisa was from Cuba and was at the hospital alone; her parents couldn't come with her. Lisa had clubbed feet and the doctors performed surgery. She was hospitalized for months and wore braces on both legs. I was only sixteen myself, but I saw the sadness and loneliness in little Lisa's eyes. It became "my job" to make Lisa feel better so she could heal and go back to Cuba. "After taking care of my sister and Lisa, nothing else mattered to me except becoming a nurse," I told Patty.

She looked at me and said, "Never, never lose that passion you're feeling about your profession. We get tired and lose sight of the main reason we became nurses — to heal, to mend and to believe we are doing a good job."

Nurses need to strive for unity and empower one another so that our voices can be heard and we can continue to shape the future of our profession.

CHAPTER TWENTY-THREE

Graduation II

It was a gorgeous evening in June when Gary, the kids and I headed to Tufts University where my graduation ceremony was being held. I felt triumphant. This was a major accomplishment for me. I thought back to the days when I was so sick from drugs and my nursing license was taken away. I had come so far, yet I would never let myself forget those years of loneliness and how I escaped reality. Remembering helped me become the nurse and the human being I was, full of compassion and understanding. This new license as an RN was a gift from God. He gave me my life back and a second chance.

My dad took a picture of me with Gary and the kids. Jessie stood proudly beside me, all dressed up and smiling and Dan was behind me, peeking his head around the corner of my ever-blossoming abdomen. I said my goodbyes to some of my instructors. I even shook hands with "Ms. Battle-ax," because my father kept eyeballing me as if he were saying, "Make peace with her." My parents took us out to eat afterward. It was a small gathering because the following week they were having a big party for me at their house.

On the way home that night, my Mom said, "Katie, remember when you were little and I told you the story about *The Little Engine That Could?*"

This was the story my Mom would tell me about the little engine that couldn't make it up the hill because it was small, not as big as the other engines that could fly up the hill! But with perseverance, the little engine kept saying, "I CAN MAKE IT. I CAN MAKE IT!" And it did, the engine persevered and reached its goal.

"Yes, Ma, I remember," I said.

"Well, Kate," she replied, "you're that little engine. I knew you could make it. I knew you could reach the top. I felt that way too when you were beginning your recovery from drugs; it was a struggle for you but I knew you'd do it."

She hugged me and said, "I am so very, very proud of you!"

A month later, I was once again with all my colleagues of the "class of '85" to take our state board examinations at the Trade Center in Boston. In order to practice as a registered nurse, you must pass the state boards. Therefore, these exams were very important. I had taken an intense one-week review course that covered everything that would be on the exams, as well as test taking skills.

The exam was two days in length and some of the questions were pretty difficult because two answers could have been the right answer; when you narrowed down the multiple-choice questions it was a guessing game. I had to laugh at some of the questions and their simplicity and the obviousness of the answers. One question I almost laughed at uncontrollably. It went something like this:

> Mary had a colostomy performed secondary to her Chron's disease. What would Mary's appropriate reaction be to her colostomy one week after surgery?
>
> 1. Mary states she's depressed and doesn't want to learn to change her colostomy bag, ever.
> 2. Mary verbalized her sadness but felt hopeful she could learn to be independent in the care of her colostomy.
> 3. Mary stated that she and Freddie (Freddie being her colostomy) would go home soon and she was thrilled to be going home with Freddie!
> 4. Mary stated she was refusing to ever change her colostomy bag and her husband would have to be in charge of it.

I was too tired, I became giddy and wished I could share this question with one of my classmates! I started to howl to myself. *Oh, boy I wonder what the answer is. DUH! Good luck with Freddy! And on # 4, I bet her husband can't wait!* This question actually helped; it got me out of the lethargic mood I was slipping into and my laughter woke me up enough to finish the exam and do pretty well the first day.

It was a long summer waiting for the results. At one point, I asked my boss, Mary, if I failed the exam, could I work as an LPN. Mary said, "Oh, honey, you'll pass."

Mary was my "Oh, honey" boss. Mary always called everyone honey or sweetie. When I first met her, I said to myself, *Is she for real?*

Is she phony or sincere? But Mary was definitely sincere. She was kind and good, with a basic love for everyone. She had a tremendous faith in God, which showed in her daily life and how she treated people. Mary said to me, "Katie, you're a beautiful person inside and out. God won't let you down."

And He didn't. On September 7th, I received notification in the mail. "Candidate Passed" is what it said. My mother told me to call her the minute I heard. I was crying "happy tears" as I tell my kids. But when my mother answered the phone and I said, "I passed."

She said. 'Who is this? I hate crank calls.'

I said, "No, Ma. It's me, Kate. I passed my boards."

"Oh, Kate, I didn't understand you. I thought it was another crank caller," she said. "Well come on over and celebrate!"

CHAPTER TWENTY-FOUR

Changes

My new job title brought a few changes for me as a professional. I could now give intravenous medications, do a full admission on patients and be in charge. In the big professional picture little really changed, only my status. No one looked at me differently, respected me more or knew how proud I felt. As an LPN, I always took on as much responsibility as I could, so the change was very subtle, and I found being in charge of the floor was only a headache. It meant only fifty cents more an hour and the charge nurse had to oversee the staff nurses, know all the patients on the floor, be responsible for doing the assignment (which most staff complained about) and also make sure all the doctors' written orders were carried out. And a really good charge nurse gets out on the floor and helps the staff nurses and aides with their patients.

For the first month I was in charge, I was excited and thrilled by my new position. After a while, though, the novelty wore off and I liked having my own assignment, own patients and no one bothering me. I was also eight months pregnant, and my pregnancy was becoming my focus since school was out and passing my boards.

A pregnant nurse is looked at totally different by patients, especially male patients. They are so fearful you're going to hurt yourself or go into labor before their very eyes that they get nervous when you're caring for them. I told Mr. Johnson I needed to give him a boost up in the bed one evening with another nurse. "No!" he screamed. "You shouldn't even be working, never mind lifting me up in the bed!"

I said jokingly, "Gee, Mr. Johnson, why don't you tell my husband that?"

Women patients were entirely different; most had the attitude of I did it; you can do it. No sympathy there! I remembered a nurse I worked with in 1980. She was nine months along in her pregnancy, ready to deliver at any moment. At 10 p.m. one night, a patient's call light went on. I walked in the room to find Lorraine sitting on the floor surrounded by water. The patient, Mr. Devaney, was perspiring and screaming, "Get her help."

"Oh, my God! Your water broke," I said.

This was Lorraine's fifth pregnancy and she said, "Oh, Kate, for crying out loud. I dropped the water container, slipped and lost my balance. My water didn't break."

We both laughed, but Mr. Devaney thought he was the cause of Lorraine's fall!

"I never want a pregnant nurse taking care of me again," he exclaimed.

My son, Chris, was born in November of 1985. I had a couple of months off and time to think about my career. I needed a change and more of a challenge than floor nursing. When I returned to work in January, I started looking at job postings. I thought working in the Intensive Care Unit or Recovery Room would be interesting, but they wanted experienced help — a nurse who had already worked in these areas. The months went by and I was restless at work but didn't know what to do next. The jobs I applied for hadn't panned out.

I had taken care of a patient named Bernie a year before and I had become friendly with him and his wife, Barbara. He had major surgery and recovered nicely. He was the owner of a restaurant in Cape Cod and invited us to dinner.

I thought a day away would help me put work in the right perspective. So, at the beginning of April we got a babysitter and headed to the Cape for an overnight. We met Barbara and Bernie at their restaurant. Bernie said, "Order anything on the menu. It's on the house." He also sent over a bottle of champagne.

Gary said, "Don't order anything expensive."

I said, "Why? Barbara and Bernie don't care."

"It's not etiquette to do that," my husband said.

"Okay, Ms. Manners," I replied. After two glasses of champagne, the waiter came over to get our order.

Gary said, "I'll have the lobster."

I looked at Gary in total astonishment, started to laugh and said, "Don't order anything expensive, its not etiquette."

Barbara and Bernie sent over another bottle of champagne and Gary said, "Boy, you must have been really nice to these people."

After dinner, when we were working on the second bottle of champagne and my husband had too much, Barbara and Bernie came over to chat. Gary said, "Thanks a lot for everything, Bert and Ernie."

I nudged him with my elbow and through gritted teeth I said, "Barbara and Bernie! You're watching way too much Sesame Street!"

CHAPTER TWENTY-FIVE

The Journey

After our short sojourn at the Cape, I returned to work feeling revitalized and renewed. I felt as if I should look around for a new job slowly. What was the rush? I had a new outlook.

Then my dad died suddenly. He was working in his garden and had been puttering around planting all afternoon. At about 5pm., my mom called him in for dinner and he had a massive heart attack. The paramedics attempted CPR but it was for naught, he was dead on arrival at Mt. Auburn hospital.

My dad's journey on this earth was completed. My father was very religious, a good Catholic, and he believed he would be rewarded and go to heaven. I believed that as well. Whatever the lessons he needed to learn on this Earth, he completed them and was starting a new journey. I would miss him tremendously.

My rocky relationship with him in my teen years and early twenties led to an acceptance and understanding as I became a mother. Watching my dad become a grandfather to my children, I found a respect for him and as he became older and I realized in my early parenting years what a difficult job being a parent could be.

As the black limousine pulled away from the church with all seven children inside and my mother nestled between my two brothers, Denise, the youngest, said, "Dad was so proud of you, Katie, for getting your RN. He told me only a couple of weeks ago."

I wished my dad could have said those words to me, but that generation found it difficult to express their feelings. He'd ever hugged me, either. Sure, as a kid, I remember the hugs and kisses, but as I got older, it stopped, probably because he thought I was too old and didn't need the affection anymore. But as I reflected on my dad, I realized he hugged all of us with his eyes. The way his Irish eyes twinkled and lit up his face when he smiled. That was the best he could do and actions speak louder than words.

He knew me better than I knew myself! He realized I needed to go to nursing school and that I had what it took. He never gave up on me, and now he was gone and I never got to tell him that.

After his burial, I went back to work a week later. Nothing would be the same. I looked at life and death differently. Even though I had dealt with death in the hospital, this was different — it was my dad. I started to value life so much more, each day was precious, a gift from God. I looked at my life, my husband and my children differently. We were all vulnerable to death and not in control of our destiny.

Three months later, I went to Seattle with my mom to visit my sister, Irene. When I returned to work, the restless feeling returned. A change was inevitable; I had to move on. But to what?

I left my staff position on 6 west and joined the per diem pool. This was a position in which the nurse received more money, chose the day and hours to work but had to go anywhere in the hospital, floating from floor to floor, wherever a nurse was needed.

The change was good. When Chris turned a year old, I worked more day shifts, which I loved. Occasionally, I'd float into the Intensive Care or Cardiac Care Unit. The patients were much sicker there and needed one-on-one nursing care, which I didn't mind. What I did mind was all the machinery — ventilators, EKG's, and other life-saving devices. I found myself fixing the machinery as a buzzer went off, intravenous lines, several of them, making sure they were running properly, etc. There was so much equipment I almost forgot there was a patient there! I felt like I was more of a mechanic or engineer. And the patients were too sick for me.

One man I took care of was intubated (a tube going into his airway to breath for him) and he was hooked up to a ventilator. He would die without this machinery. But he was awake, and his big brown eyes were staring at me. His frightened eyes saying, "Help."

A year later, while working on 7 central, which was a neurological floor, I took care of a man who had been at a dinner function at a local restaurant and suffered a heart attack while eating his dinner. He hadn't been resuscitated quickly enough and was brain dead when he got to the Emergency Room. He was in a coma when I took care of him. Flaccid, unable to move, the nurses had to turn and position him frequently, suction the secretions from his lungs so he wouldn't get pneumonia and try to just keep him comfortable. He was dying; there was no hope. I watched the family arrive day after day, expecting miracles. It was a large devoted family much like my own.

As I was preparing him to be transferred to a nursing home, I realized this could have been my dad, and I was so grateful it was not. He would have hated to linger, being suctioned, depending on someone else to take care of him. A quick, painless heart attack is really the way to go.

I told my mom the story about this patient. She was grateful my dad died the way he did, but my mother had an anxious look on her face. "What's wrong, Ma?" I asked.

She told me the story. "Before your father died, he grabbed his chest and yelled, 'Mary.' I ran over and thought I could save him. I shook him and shook him and his head fell back, I saw he had a piece of gum, a Chiclets, that was down his throat."

"So, what did you do," I asked.

She replied, "I stuck my finger down his throat to grab the Chiclets but I hit his throat."

I looked over and I knew she was thinking that she somehow caused him to choke.

"Look, Ma," I said, "Dad died of a heart attack. Chiclets or no Chiclets, he would have died. He wasn't breathing, so his piece of gum was not the cause of his death nor were you."

She agreed and looked relieved. We both started laughing because my father loved chewing Chiclets! There was always a piece in his mouth. Every night after dinner, my mum or dad would pass around the Chiclets box and we'd all take a piece. It was family thing, a family ritual.

I said, "Ma, Dad died doing what he loved, chewing a Chiclets!!"

CHAPTER TWENTY-SIX

Drgs

DRGs or Diagnostic Related Groups was a billing system adopted in the 1980s by the Federal Medicare program in which hospital procedures are rated in terms of cost, after which a standard flat rate is set per procedure. Medicare claims for those procedures are paid in that amount, regardless of the cost to the hospital."

For instance, if a patient needed gall bladder surgery, the DRGs rate per gall bladder surgery may be $5,000, which would include the whole hospitalization. Great, if it was simple surgery. But what if it wasn't and the patient needed to go back for more surgery due to a complication? The hospital wouldn't be allowed to charge for more services and they would get stuck with the extra cost. The virtue of the DRG system was that it simplified billing and gave hospitals the incentive to cut costs by setting limits on what they were allowed to charge.

To me, DRGs threw a curve ball into the medical profession and that's when everything started to change. Hospital administrations became nervous and started cutting costs, and of course the nursing department was the first to be addressed. The Director of Nurses had a meeting with the per diem staff. We were told they would try to use us but would depend more on the staff nurses, and our hours would be cut. Bottom line, I needed to find another job. Were patients affected? Of course they were. Less staff decreased nursing care. Did the hospitals care? Of course, but they had to cut corners and the per diem pool was the first to go.

It was hard to find another job because all healthcare facilities were affected by DRGs. I landed a non-benefited per diem position with a for-profit visiting nurse establishment. I was paid per visit to go into patients' homes and change dressings, give intravenous medications, monitor blood pressures, etc. This was similar work to what was done in a hospital but the patients were in their own homes. Patients were being discharged quickly from hospitals, so the acuity was still there. I felt these patients were being discharged too soon from hospitals; they would go home not stabilized, tubes still in and feeling vulnerable.

I took care of two young quadriplegic men in their late 20s, Mike and Tom. Mike, a carpenter, fell off a second story scaffold and became paralyzed; Tom was drunk, jumped out of a car when it was moving and was paralyzed from cervical injuries. Both had skin breakdowns (decubitus ulcers) and needed their wounds dressed daily.

The first day I walked into Tom's house, he looked at me strangely. After changing his dressing, I said, "Tom is something wrong?"

He said, "Well, I was hoping for a much younger nurse."

"Hmm, I always thought 38 were pretty young," I replied. *What a blow to my ego!* "Oh, well, Tom, the world is full of middle-aged women. Get used to it!" Fortunately, he wasn't on caseload long; his wound healed and I never saw him again.

Michael, I got close to. He couldn't accept the fact that he had to spend the rest of his life in a wheelchair. So, he drank and he drank his troubles away. After six months of caring for him and doing daily wound care, he disappeared. His mom came from Florida and was there two hours, packed his things up and they headed south.

I would get an occasional shift at Laureat, but not much more than that. A two-day position opened at a Boston Hospital in the Recovery Room and I took it. I realized how much I hated it after a month; all the surgery was from the neck up! Eyes, ears, nose and throat. Yuck!

I assisted a doctor one day while he put medication (with a long 3" needle) above the patient's eye to numb it for surgery and almost passed out. The patient did better than I did!

One evening, a sixty-year-old man came into the recovery room after having a radical neck dissection. This is where the doctors remove all the cancerous tumors in the lymph nodes and surrounding structures. Mr. Johns had a laryngectomy as well because of cancer. When he came to me, he had a tube coming out of his neck with dressings covering both sides. He started bleeding right through the dressings a half hour after he came to the Recovery Room. His neck was swelling and a collection of blood (hematoma) was pressing on his airway, so he was rushed back into surgery.

After a year of trying to make myself like this job, I quit. Laureat was starting to use per diem nurses again on a regular basis so I took a contract position (meaning I'd only work on that particular floor) on 7 central four days a week. I let out a sigh of relief, hoping the DRGs wouldn't affect my job status again.

CHAPTER TWENTY-SEVEN

My Awakening

I had always been interested in near death experiences. Although the thought of someone dying then returning to earth frightened me, I was too interested in the subject to let fear take over. I read a few books on near death experiences, even watched TV programs. There was definitely something to this phenomenon.

Remembering some of my patients in the past, like Carmen when he had a cardiac arrest and said he was on the ceiling watching us, I wondered if there was more to it. One evening when I was on duty, I took care of a patient named Jack who'd had back surgery. I read his history from his chart and saw that he'd had a cardiac arrest four years before. He was only 50 now! Later on when I was making his bed, he started talking about his past hospitalizations. "I had a heart attack four years ago and it changed my life," Jack said.

"How?" I asked.

Jack stated he had always been self-centered, lived in a narcissistic manner and always had to be center stage. "God was not in my consciousness, I had no belief in anything but myself. I didn't hurt anyone, but I didn't ever help anyone either," he said.

Jack continued telling me that one afternoon he was at a friend's house playing pool. He was about to hit the eight ball in the corner pocket when he keeled over from chest pains. The next thing he knew he was near heaven. God was there and the whole experience was magnificent. God graciously showed him how to live in his light. "I was told I had to go back to Earth. I wanted to stay, but the next thing I knew it was two days later and my friend was standing over me in the Cardiac Care Unit. Tubes were everywhere and the only thing I could think of was that I wanted to go back to heaven." Jack said the experience changed him, and now his world is centered around God and living by the Golden Rule: Do unto others as you would have them do unto you.

The following month another patient told me he died four times and went to heaven and came back. "Every time I begged to stay. It's more beautiful than what you could ever imagine, but for some reason God wants me here," he said.

One weekend I took care of an elderly woman named Annie. She'd had hip surgery and was recovering nicely. Annie said to me, "I'm dying. I'll be dead by tomorrow night."

"No, Annie," I said, "you're getting better. You're not dying."

Before I left work that afternoon, I went to say goodbye to Annie. Her daughter was there and she was crying. She said her mother was confused, talking "Ragtime."

Suddenly, Annie yelled out, "Pete, I'll be with you soon. See, Katie? Pete is over there behind the door."

I looked at her daughter, Caroline, and said, "Who's Pete?"

She said, "Pete's my dad. He's been dead for two years."

The doctors thought Annie was confused because of an electrolyte imbalance. Blood was drawn and tested, but all her laboratory results were within normal limits.

The next day around noon, Annie complained of chest pain. A couple of doctors arrived, medications were given and vital signs monitored but they couldn't find anything wrong. Annie died at 6 p.m. that evening.

These true stories and more, made me realize I had been living behind a curtain. Every once in a while, I'd peek around the curtain, become afraid of the unknown and slip back behind it. These episodes with my patients became a true awakening into another world for me, showing me the meaning of life and what it meant to be on a spiritual journey. We are on an earthly mission; there are lessons to be learned and challenges to be faced with hope and faith as our road map. The fear was gone, death had a new meaning; it was the end, yet the beginning of something new.

CHAPTER TWENTY-EIGHT

No Respect

I started to branch out a bit with my role as an RN, learning about alternative medicines. I took a course in "REIKI" which is a natural healing method that uses the hands of a healer to channel energy to another person through energy centers, known as "chakras" in the body. Reiki is actually a very old practice and has been used for thousands of years. It was reintroduced in the 1800s by Mikao Usui in Japan.

After taking Reiki I and II, I became a practitioner myself and would perform Reiki on some of my patients. It has a calming effect and can restore balance to the body, supporting the body's natural ability to heal itself. Reiki is not intended to be a cure, but is used along with traditional medicine.

I also decided not to work at the hospital as much and work as an RN for two local school systems. I had the opportunity to help care for (even enlighten) our next generation: teenagers. Some of these kids are in such desperate need of attention and the only way they get it is through physical ailments. Sure, there are those who arrive in the nurse's office with real physical problems, but most show up with vague symptoms like a headache, stomachache or they have cramps from their period. But how do you detect if they're really sick?

A student showed up chewing gum, acting cool, fresh, and said, "I got cramps." So, I have her lie down, wondering if she's trying to get out of class. Her temperature was normal and there was no physical reason she should be hanging around the nurse's office.

"You can go back to class Charlene," I said.

She cringed. "Can I lie down for a few minutes?"

"Okay. For few minutes," I said.

Then the story unfolds. "Am I too young to have sex? I feel lonely; my parents are never around."

So, I sat and talked, and helped her sort her problems out. She needed someone to talk to. There were many, many Charlenes and Charles and Donnas with these same issues. What they needed most was love and nurturing, and someone to validate their feelings. What I wanted to do was hug each kid, fill him or her with love, but of course, you can't. You'd probably be sued if you touched a student.

One morning, a fifteen-year-old girl showed up really sick. I called her mother and she wasn't home. "Who else can I call?" I asked.

"My sister, Stacey, is a senior. She gets out of class at twelve because she has a baby."

"How old is Stacey?" I asked.

"Seventeen."

"She's too young, I can't release you with her," I said. "Why don't you rest awhile and see if you feel better?"

Her sister Stacey showed up anyway at twelve o'clock and I explained the situation.

"But I'm a mother," she said.

"Look," I said, "do you have an aunt or uncle I can call?"

"No," Stacey said. "There's only my mother and she's never around."

God, I thought, *what a responsibility for Stacey.* She was pregnant at 15 and had a two-year-old. It reminded me of the movie we saw in nursing school called, "Babies Having Babies," a film on middle school and high school pregnancies. I wanted to cry for these two girls! Then I thought, *How do the permanent nurses stand it, day after day dealing with the physical and emotional problems of teenagers?* And they were paid peanuts!

I believe school nurses are not respected enough within the school system, and society sees school nurses as sitting in an office, giving out aspirin. No way! There have been so many changes within the schools that nurses play a major role in a student's life. Since inclusion (which means the right to belong to the mainstream, where all students, from the learning disabled to the ones with physical problems, are joined together in the classroom regardless of their disability) changed the nurse's role and made it even more challenging. Sometimes I wonder if this is a realistic approach to teaching our children. Many of the handicapped students, who may have been in other schools or hospitalized, were now mainstreaming with other "normal" kids. This has impacted the lives of teachers and nurses immensely.

I found myself suctioning a student one day. (He had a chronic respiratory problem that required a tracheotomy.) He had a portable suction machine and came down to the nurse's office if he needed secretions removed from his airway so he could breath. He was very bright and fit in intellectually, but needed his physical needs met. Another with a tube going into her stomach needed tube feedings at lunchtime. All students were included, and it was a big adjustment for all school systems.

Then there were the vision and hearing screenings performed once a year on all students in this particular system. I started at one school and worked my way up to the high school. What an eye opener! One day while doing a vision screening, a 2nd grader named Kaitlin was crying. She was standing in line, waiting with the other students and they were making fun of her. She was wearing mismatched clothes and two different shoes.

I said to the other nurse working with me, "What is the background on Kaitlin?"

"Poverty," Sandy said. "Four kids in the family, mother works, father left, and the mom is trying to stay out of the welfare system."

Then there was Mark. I substituted a couple of days at a middle school. One 8th grade boy named Mark repeatedly appeared at the nurse's office. *Boy*, I thought, *he looks a lot older than 8th grade*. Come to find out Mark was 15, almost 16. He had stayed back in school twice for not passing and getting into trouble. He had a headache and wanted to go home. I sent him back to class twice after examining him and finding nothing wrong.

The third time he appeared I said, "Mark, what else is wrong?"

"I just hate school. I'm going to quit when I turn 16," he said.

The sad part was Mark was a bright kid, he just got lost somewhere along the way. But who failed him? Parents, teachers, society in general?

He was giving up and I was afraid the system would give up on him as well and he would be in jail in another year. When I called his mother to pick him up, she said, "Can't. I'm heading out. Call his grandmother."

Over the last several years, there has been a dramatic change in the role of the school nurse. They are the only health professionals many children see regularly. They care for increasing numbers of children affected by chronic ailments such as substance abuse, eating disorders and teen pregnancy. Nationally there are 86,000 public schools but only about 60,000 school nurses to meet the needs of 46 million children, 20 million with chronic medical conditions.

What can be done to improve the nurse's role? Public awareness with other health care professionals, school systems and parents helping to improve the conditions for the school nurse such as considering nurse-to-student ratio, pay raises to be equal to other health care professionals, such as nurses in a hospital setting and for school administrators to provide the safest possible environment. Maybe with this awareness and validation of their profession, school nurses will receive the respect they most certainly deserve.

CHAPTER TWENTY-NINE

Is This For Real?

A two-day evening position opened up in day surgery at Laureat. Debbie, the Nurse Manager of the unit, who had also graduated from LPN school with me, offered me the position. I took it. Between two days there and doing some per diem and private duty, I was all set financially.

Day surgery, for all intents and purposes, is for patients who have surgeries that don't require an overnight stay in the hospital, such as breast biopsies, knee arthroscopies and cardiac catheterizations to name a few. Many of these patients were healthy to begin with and I thought I died and went to heaven with this job. No bedpans! No bed baths! No debilitating illnesses! Yippee! After my initial orientation, I said to one of the nurses, "Is this for real? I love this job. People actually get up and go home the same day."

The most powerful force, the one aspect of my job that I loved, was the staff. When I started working there in 1994, everyone seemed happy and content. It was two large rooms with state-of-the-art medical equipment, one pre-operative room and one post-operative room. Each nurse had her own assignment and her own patients but we all worked together and helped one another out.

The pre-op side had twelve slots for twelve patients awaiting surgery. We would start intravenous lines, obtain blood samples, make sure all their pre-operative testing was done such as blood work and x-rays, and make sure all results were visible for the surgeons and anesthesiologists. Sometimes, one or all of the above were missing. The nurses and support staff would have to track the results down. I felt like an investigator at times!

Doctors would become frantic "Where is so and so's x-ray or lab work?" Or the blood work was not within normal limits! "Why wasn't I notified? Get more blood work now," the doctors would say. The nurse's job was to get it done, completed and left at the bedside.

The post-operative side was where the patients recovered after surgery. We'd monitor their respiratory status, taking blood pressure, pulse and breathing rate as well as their temperature every fifteen minutes. We'd also check their surgical sites and slowly recover them, until the patient was ready to leave. Frequently, we had to find an overnight bed because of a complication the patient might be having. But a good part of the time the patients recovered for a few hours and went home with instructions.

I worked 1 p.m. to 9:30 p.m. My hours overlapped the day shift and I was able to learn what happened during those hours. The staff got along well. We always seemed to be laughing and joking about something. Sometimes, if a patient wasn't doing well, or if we were extremely busy, tempers would flare and we tended to yell or be short with one another. But as quickly as we yelled, it would be over. It was an accepted emotion because of the nature of our job.

The surgeons, especially for the first surgery of the day, would be intense. They could be very short tempered and unkind. But somehow, we overlooked these shortcomings and held no offense, because if they yelled it really wasn't directed toward you, it was more toward the impending surgery and the necessity to do a good job. Apologies never occurred.

One of my first emergencies was with a 39-year-old man, a jogger who had a knee arthroscopy. He came back from surgery with a pulse of 52. Low, but not really because he was a runner; most joggers have low pulses. But five minutes later, he became sweaty and pale, and his pulse was 36. I quickly called the anesthesiologist and gave the patient .04 milligrams of atropine, a drug that increases the heart rate. His pulse slowly rose up to 48 but he required more atropine, which the anesthesiologist administered. His heart rate plateau was at 60, Phew!! I hoped that didn't happen again.

I had a 70-year-old lady who underwent a breast biopsy because a suspicious area was detected on a mammogram the week before. The surgeon wanted a definitive diagnosis with the biopsy. The patient, Millie, had not been feeling well for the past year and had increased hair loss all over her body. She only had a few wisps of hair on her head, and no arm, leg or pubic hair was noted. The cause? The doctors weren't sure.

Millie arrived in the post-op area and was groggy from the anesthesia. When I hooked her up to the EKG monitor I noticed she had tattoos on her upper right breast of a woman on a motorcycle, and on her left shoulder the name "Jack" was tattooed surrounded by a big heart. Millie slowly woke up, and was laughing, cracking jokes, and making fun of her hairless body!

Half an hour later, I sat Millie on the edge of the bed and noticed another tattoo. It was a "mouse" right above her right groin. She saw me looking at it. She started laughing and said, "Can you believe that mouse ate my pussy?" I wanted to burst out laughing, but I contained my emotions.

The next day, I told my mother the story, and she said, "That is disgraceful. She has no class!"

I said, "Ma, come on. You have to admit that was pretty funny, and considering her age and she has tattoos!"

"Well, she just wasn't brought up right. Her mother didn't do a good job."

I became angry at my mother's snobbish attitude. I said, "Mom, what exactly is the meaning of being brought up right?" I should have shut up then and didn't. I went on to say, "So, you think you brought your children up right by driving us around to mental institutions and making fun of the "crazy" people?"

The look on my mother's face made me wish I had not brought up that part of our lives. "I had my reasons, Kate. It was hard with seven kids and your dad's drinking."

"I know, Ma," I said, "but that really bothered me, those rides to Met State and McLean's. I was a scared kid."

"All your brothers and sisters thought it was fun, an outing. You were the only one afraid."

"Some outing," I replied. "Couldn't we have gone to Waverly Oaks for a picnic? That's an outing, Ma." She didn't reply but the look on her face said 'Life isn't that easy; life isn't just black and white.'

CHAPTER THIRTY

A Roller Coaster Ride

Over the months working in day surgery, I became close to two of my co-workers, Ginny and Barbara. When I first met them, none of us knew how much I was going to lean on them for emotional support. The next two years I was on an emotional roller coaster that I never thought I would get off of.

When I first met Ginny, we realized we both grew up in the same town and I graduated high school with her brother. We became immediate friends. Barbara and I were both runners and would jog together, and run in road races. Our husbands would join us occasionally for a night in Boston, and lasting friendships were formed.

Work started to change. It was almost not noticeable at first: little things were said, hints of the hospital not doing well financially. Then my old floor closed, nurses were not laid off but relocated to other floors. Six months later, the layoffs came. A couple of nurse managers were let go, that day, that minute. Their desks were cleaned out and the managers were gone. Many of us were shocked at what happened and the way it was done!

This wasn't exclusive to Laureat. Most hospitals all over the United States were feeling a financial crunch, maybe from Medicare and the effects of health maintenance organizations. Hospitals were downsizing, not hiring and there was a salary freeze. Ambulatory surgery took over the Intravenous Therapy Department. Our head nurse, Debbie, assumed responsibility for both departments. We were busier. More responsibility was given to each of us, and the amount of staff stayed the same; like it or lump it. Work became a roller coaster ride.

Sick, dehydrated patients needing IV fluids would be part of ambulatory surgery's world. Sick cancer patients would come to us once the Oncology Department closed at night to finish their course of chemotherapy. Some of these patients would physically look like they were on their last days on earth. They were skin and bones with bandanas around their heads because of hair loss. The look of determination was on their faces; the look of hope in their sunken eyes. These were the patients I had the utmost respect for. The courage and perseverance they had, not willing to give up; the cancer would not get them.

I found myself doing more and more Reiki on people. Patients were so open to hands-on healing. It felt good and helped them relax. I did Reiki on a patient one day who couldn't urinate, and couldn't go home until he did. I placed my hands on his stomach near his bladder and did Reiki. A resident doctor walked by and asked what I was doing. I explained. He looked at me and said, "That's voodoo."

Twenty minutes later, the patient urinated and was discharged. I looked at the resident and said, "My voodoo worked!"

With all the changes going on at work, my home life also felt like a tornado had hit. My two oldest children revealed to my husband and I some trauma that had happened over many years during their childhood. Because of its affect, my son, Dan, who was sixteen, needed several hospitalizations in adolescent mental institutions for posttraumatic stress.

For six months, I watched him be placed in different hospitals and rehabilitation centers. I saw on a personal level how the health care system worked and I was enraged! I was emotionally exhausted and was fortunately able to vent my frustrations with Ginny, Barbara and some of the other nurses.

I was worried about Dan's well being, and didn't know if he could emotionally survive the trauma. My life stayed on that roller coaster for another year before things began to stabilize at home and work.

Our department also became the transfer center. This meant patients would arrive from the other sites Laureat owned and stay in day surgery until a hospital bed was available. Sometimes, I felt we were getting in over our heads and it could lead to errors being made. I had been in day surgery for close to three years, and at Laureat for almost sixteen. How much more was I willing to do before I called it quits? But all hospitals were the same. Health care was changing and either I changed with it or make a career move to something else.

As my children stabilized, I felt better. I had been going for polarity therapy and thought I might learn to become a polarity therapist. Polarity is another alternative hands-on healing art that balances the energy currents in the body. I had polarity treatments for myself for six months and it helped me relax and learn how to incorporate love, positive attitudes, exercise and diet in my life.

While I wanted to be a practitioner, I realized I needed a break. My brain was on overload and I actually needed to be "the patient." I continued practicing my Reiki at work, and at home and on family members. My friend, Maureen, was one of the recipients of Reiki. Maureen was one of my closest friends for the last five years, a platonic soul mate full of light and love.

Maureen had been overweight and unhappy with herself. She started attending OA (Overeaters Anonymous) for a period of two years and lost 150 pounds! I saw her self-esteem rise as her weight decreased. I was one of her biggest fans and very proud of her!

In February of 1997, she became increasingly exhausted and went for a check up. Her mammogram was suspicious and her doctor did a breast biopsy and lymph node biopsies as well. The tests came back positive for melanoma (a form of cancer) and she had over fifty lymph nodes surgically removed. She was hopeful for recovery through the spring but as summer approached, she started to swell with fluid in her abdomen, hands and feet.

Her radiation treatments were over and she had been so positive that the cancer was gone. We agreed I would do Reiki once a week. Maureen would lie on her bed as I started the treatment. My hands went to her head first, then her old incision line, her abdomen, hands and feet, wherever I felt she needed it. Maureen was such a trooper. She'd take the focus off herself and say, "Tell me how Jess and Dan are doing," and she was the best listener, a true friend.

One week, as I was doing a treatment she said, "Do you think there is hope for me, Kate?"

I would get mad at her and say, "You're not dying, Maureen!" And I would think selfishly, *I'm not ready for you to die.* I was in somewhat of a denial state because the melanoma was slowly taking over her body, like PacMan, chewing up the good tissue a mile a minute, progressing too quickly. I was losing my friend, my buddy, and on some level I was not realizing it.

One very warm day toward the end of July, I went over Maureen's to Reiki her. I placed my hands on her abdomen and actually felt the negativity of the cancer. I said to myself, *Maureen is dying.* I went every day to her house, Reikied her, talked and just visited.

She said, "I really want to go to the beach, I need to see the ocean." She had reached a level of acceptance with her disease. She knew she was dying. I made the decision that she was too weak. I was afraid to take her to the beach, afraid of what could happen. Two years later, I wished I had taken her, wished I could have delivered her last request to see the ocean.

She was admitted to Mass General on August 10th and died on August 12th surrounded by family and friends, and Reiki practitioners who placed their hands on her body, helping her with the transition of leaving this world and going on to the next. I looked into her stone blue eyes one last time and realized I was losing one of the best friends I'd ever had.

Reiki didn't save Maureen's life, nor did surgery or radiation, but I passionately believe that Maureen was helped through Reiki with the emotional acceptance of her illness and her peaceful exit from this world.

CHAPTER THIRTY-ONE

Had Enough

I finally got to the point where I had enough of hospital nursing. The rat race was over. I made a pact with myself that I would never ever work in a hospital again. Laureat had been good to me and in turn I had been good to Laureat. But now I was divorcing myself, moving on. To what? All hospitals and health care facilities were troubled. Some hospitals were merging with others so they wouldn't close. Other smaller facilities were closing their doors; they couldn't keep up with their financial obligations. My husband asked me to rethink my decision about quitting my job. But I knew I had to make a change or I would stay miserable; I was physically, emotionally and mentally exhausted. As I walked out the front doors of Laureat on my last day, I felt frightened; I was leaving a place that had been my home for sixteen years. My life was comfortable and predictable. A world-renowned facility that had strengthened my skills and helped me be the nurse I was today. But it was the end and a time for a new beginning.

I found a job, full time day shift at a local visiting nurse association. I had done VNA before and knew the ropes; the money, hours and territory I would be going to were perfect. My supervisor, Maureen, wanted me to have a good orientation even though I wasn't totally green; she assigned me to be with a nurse (preceptor) every day for two weeks. She showed me everything, explaining the nature of my job from soup to nuts.

The first day I went out with a nurse named Joan. She met me at the office with her red sports car; her personality and mine clicked and we became immediate friends; kindred spirits after talking for ten minutes. Joan was tall, over 5'10" and ran around like a chicken with her head cut off! Lots and lots of energy and a great sense of humor to boot!

She hopped in her red sports car outside the office and said, "Okay, Kate, follow me." Joan was not your stereotypical nurse. I could hear her music blaring, see her dancing around, pictured her making a corner in her sports car on two wheels. When we arrived at the first patient's house Joan said, "Before we go in let me tell you about finding the houses on a street; all the even numbers are on the right, the odd numbers are on the left."

I burst out laughing and said, "No shit, Joan! I've known that since about kindergarten." That humor, our similar personalities found us laughing, sometimes uncontrollably throughout the day. Before we went into each patient's house Joan would tell me about their medical history; a brief synopsis that would enlighten me as to why we were going in there.

The third house we went into was at a local housing project. The patient was a 76-year-old female, had lost her husband a year before and depended on her dog, "Virgil" for companionship. She had been discharged from the hospital the previous day to rule out a heart attack — we were monitoring her blood pressure, teaching her about her medications and making sure she was following her low salt diet. Her name was Peggy. "Just call me 'the Pegster'" she said. "That's what Frankie used to call me." (Frankie was her dead husband.)

"Ooh … Kaaay," I said as I looked around her cluttered living room for a place to sit, but Virgil kept jumping up and licking me, looking for attention as "the Pegster" cried about her beloved Frankie.

"Let me show you his picture," she said as she unsteadily walked over to the wall, grabbed his photo off the wall, clutching it, becoming more and more short of breath as her 4'10" 240 pound frame clumsily walked back to Joan and me. Frankie, to me, looked like a philanderer; it was a picture of him at a wedding, all dolled up, hair slicked back, mustache curled up, a devilish grin adorning his face and his arm draped around one of the bridesmaids. "He was so devoted to me," Peg said. Joan and I both looked at each other with that 'don't you dare laugh' look. Joan went in the other room to check Peg's medication and Virgil, the dog, followed her.

I heard Joan say from the other room, "Okay, doggie, off my leg." I peeked in the kitchen to see Virgil attached to Joan's leg, humping away! She was shaking him off but he was staying attached! Joan finally yelled, "Can someone please help me in here?"

Finally, Peg got up, went to the kitchen and said, "Virgil, knock that shit off."

Grinning, I said to myself, *Oh no. Is this what home care is all about?*

Two weeks later, I was on my own, with a territory north of Boston that covered four towns. I loved the autonomy, being alone, not having to answer to anyone. One of the very first patients I had was a 48-year-old named Joe. He was diagnosed with juvenile diabetes at the age of seven, lost his eyesight at 25, could still see shadows and faces but most everything was blurry. In May of 1997, he had a kidney and pancreatic transplant and had run into complications of wound infections.

When I saw him in July, the nurses were doing wound care to his infected abdomen. Normal saline, wet to dry dressings twice a day. Then he had developed ulcers on both heels, so dressing changes had to be done to those as well.

Prior to his surgery, Joe had always maintained a level of independence. He had been a schoolteacher and worked in the business world, and now he missed being around people. Before his surgery, he would catch the bus outside of his house and go into Boston. Cane in hand, he would walk Newbury Street, go to the Boston Public Library, sit somewhere and have coffee, listen to the sounds of life. Joe told me he wanted that back, to be able to walk out his door and hop on the #350 bus to Boston. He would get discouraged and feel as if he would never get better. Joe was one of the most courageous patients I ever had.

Some days I'd walk in his house and see the sad look on his face, the look of 'this is never going to end. Is it?' So, I would try to make him laugh and tell him about all my other patients. He loved hearing my stories.

One day, he said, "Kate, you need to write a book about your patients. I'm telling you it will be a best seller!" Joe knew the life stories of every nurse who saw him, and he would pass on their life stories to the other nurses. We all knew about one another's lives through Joe. It was a coming together of all the healers in Joe's life.

I remember walking into the office one day and Diane, another RN who saw Joe every evening, said, "When are you leaving for Lake Placid?"

I said, "Did I tell you I was going to Lake Placid?"

"No, Joe did. He said your son was in a hockey tournament before Christmas!" And that's how it went, bits and pieces of each other's lives, and we all had a common goal. Get Joe well enough to hop on the #350 bus, so he could go into Boston.

After eight months of being a visiting nurse and going into people's homes, I started to get lonely. "Wouldn't it be fun to do this and have a partner?" I said to Joan one day.

"Sure, Kate. Great idea, but I'm sure Medicare would hate that idea!"

I found myself striking up conversations with the most unlikely people — a teenager in Dunkin' Donuts, a UPS driver who had stopped for coffee at a convenience store, etc. I missed having people around and other nurses to talk to. The radio stations were becoming very old very quickly. I criticized every disc jockey! Howard Stern! No, thanks. Why was he on WBCN anyway? Whatever happened to Charles Laquadera?

I would call radio stations while I was on the road and try to get through to win a contest. I was bored driving from house to house. I cried over the book, "Mists of Avalon," that I listened to on tape, and wanted to marry Sir Lancelot by the end of the story.

When I was at VNA a year, our company was hit. There were layoffs. Several nurses and administrators were let go, sent off to the world of collecting unemployment. The staff that stayed, including me, had to take a pay cut and benefits were cut.

I tried to understand and figure out why this was happening. Was it because of Medicare Reform? Yes, of course, partly. Did our health maintenance organizations play a role in downsizing? Absolutely. Were medical costs too high, supply companies greedy, medications too expensive? I didn't know the answers. Those were only rumors. But I wanted to find out and figure out why my medical profession, our politicians and insurance companies were failing in keeping patients and us employed from obtaining the optimum care they deserved.

CHAPTER THIRTY-TWO

HMOs

Health maintenance organizations (HMOs) represent "prepaid" or "capitates" insurance plans in which individuals or their employers pay a fixed monthly fee for services instead of a separate charge for each visit or service. Depending on the type of HMO, services may be provided in a central facility or in a physician's own office.

Many health care workers and people in general are against managed care and look at it as mismanaged care because of some of the drawbacks. HMOs claim to provide access to a full range of benefits such as hospital and outpatient services, x-rays, laboratory work and even rehabilitation therapy as well as home care services. Those against HMOs claim most of these services are limited and the HMO member can only select certain primary care physicians. The elderly hear the words "we will pay for your medications" from these senior health plans and think it's a golden opportunity, but they don't understand the whole package.

Many senior citizens who had dropped their Medicare coverage to join senior plan HMOs have become very disappointed. Elderly people who joined HMOs felt they were talked into dropping Medicare because "a pretty picture" was painted for them with numerous benefits, only to find they had been misguided and were not covered for certain medical costs.

At times, I was on the fence about HMOs. They appeared to take an interest in preventative medicine, offering classes on nutrition, stress management and wellness. But when the member became sick, maybe even hospitalized, the scenario changed.

I had a patient named Mary Beth with chronic respiratory problems. She was only 55 years old and was in and out of the hospital frequently because she "just couldn't breath" as she put it. Her HMO insurance limited her hospital inpatient stays and sent her home to receive visiting nurse services, only to limit them as well. After seeing Mary Beth three times one week to monitor her respiratory status, I felt she was not ready for discharge. Her HMO basically said, "Too bad, your visits are up."

Two things could happen. I could continue seeing Mary Beth until she was ready for me to discharge her and my agency would absorb the cost (which I was strongly encouraged not to do!) or Mary Beth would end up back in the hospital. *What kind of insurance is that?* I thought.

I had first hand experience with my son, Dan. He was sixteen-years-old, depressed, suicidal, needing hospitalization and I was told where my son had to go. My husband and I didn't have a choice, our HMO ruled! There were only two adolescent facilities that our insurance would send him to, so we were very limited. One hospital was so inappropriate I signed him out AMA (against medical advice). If I wanted more services, I had to go to the Department of Mental Health, which I did do. They were wonderful but over-worked and underpaid. The other option was to get him a public health bed, which is available after so many hospitalizations.

But on the flip side of HMOs, most medications are only $3-$5 and a doctor's visit also has a very low co-payment. If a person is hospitalized, they don't have to worry about their insurance only covering 80% of the hospitalization.

Dealing with HMOs is also exhausting as a nurse. I took care of a patient named Ed Brown. He was 64 years old with a diabetic history, was insulin dependent and had lost one leg because of poor circulation. Nurses were in to do wound care on his other leg so he wouldn't lose that one, too! His senior plan allowed us to visit him every day but they wanted us to teach his wife to do wound care. What insurance companies have a hard time understanding is that family members are not always available and some are not teachable! Hello?

They expect 90-year-old wives to do wound care on their 95-year-old husband? I don't think so! In Ed's case, his wife worked and was not available. I've often been concerned about how family members do the dressing changes. They forget to wash their hands and wear gloves or simply do the wound care inappropriately. The patient is just being set up for another infection!

My friend, Patty, who was an airline stewardess, was diagnosed with throat cancer last Christmas. A mother of four, she was not only worried about her surgery and recovery, she had a family to be concerned about as well. After six months of surgery then recovery, the airline dropped her HMO insurance and the HMO declined to keep her on unless she paid over $400 a month. Not only did this affect Patty's health care but her family's as well. They now have no health insurance.

Another managed care patient I had was Anthony. He was in his seventies and had switched from Medicare to a senior HMO plan. I was nervous for Anthony. He had cirrhosis of the liver and was constantly getting small bowel obstructions. He could be very ornery and would give the nurses a hard time.

He stood 5 feet tall and was very angry with his illness. His main goal was to get to the North End of Boston every Sunday for a good Italian meal. My visits were limited. I felt I had to beg his insurance company to let me make more skilled nursing visits. He needed a nurse to detect a bowel obstruction, a worsening of his cirrhosis or if his lungs were filling with fluid.

Once again, his visiting nurse services were cut off and if I saw him again the agency would absorb the cost. So, I discharged Anthony under the care of his family, knowing he'd be hospitalized in another two weeks. If I were allowed to stay on and monitor his physical status, another hospitalization could have been avoided by getting him on the right medication and diet regime.

With every HMO, there is a nurse, a case manager following the patient from hospitalization through home care and discharge. If you come upon a good case manager, you're lucky; you've won the jackpot. Visits will be approved quickly and not be too limited. If you get a bad one, the whole scenario can be hell. It's like pulling teeth to convince them that your patient NEEDS A NURSE!

Not all HMOs are bad and not all case managers are evil and mean-spirited. Some are very compassionate people, only following the rules and regulations handed down to them. Unfortunately, it is the consumer that suffers — the old, the sick, the indigent and patients too sick or confused to speak up for themselves.

Where was the case manager for my son, a sick suicidal 16-year-old? Why weren't they advocating for him? I would call our HMO begging for a better hospital and was never able to reach the right person. I would reach machines, leave messages and never get a return phone call. I felt ignored, as if our son was costing them too much money.

HMOs are for the healthy people — you, me, the baby boomers walking around taking part in wellness programs, paying their co-payments for physicals and pharmaceutical needs. Everything looking "hunky dory" until illness hits. The beginning of the end.

CHAPTER THIRTY-THREE

Medicare

Congress enacted the Medicare program in August 1965 as part of Lyndon Johnson's "Great Society." President Johnson believed that in a land as prosperous as ours, we could afford to take care of everyone; no one should be left out of the great wealth.

Medicare was added to the Social Security Act in 1965, it was designed to cover the costs of health care services and to insure access to a level of health care for the over 65 age group. Medicare has accomplished two things: coverage is available without regard to medical conditions and at the same price, based on eligibility requirements.

Thirty-five years later, politicians are worried about the Medicare program and $270 billion in Medicare funding should be cut in order to make the Medicare program sound. Medicare coverage increased from 19.1 million in 1966 to 36.7 million in 1994 — a 92% increase.

The Medicare program seems to be draining more and more dollars from the Federal budget.

Over the last few years, Medicare has had to make changes, cutbacks in order for the program to survive. The program was never intended for chronic care, only acute medical problems that involved short-term hospitalizations and outpatient care. Over the years, Medicare seemed to be covering costs of the elderly with custodial care needs (walking, getting in and out of bed, bathing, dressing and feeding). Medicare is reinforcing its need to take care of only the aged with skilled needs. This has really impacted the home health agencies. Visiting nurse associations are trying to stay within the rules and regulations of Medicare protocol and discharge patients who had been on service for many years who weren't entirely receiving skilled nursing care, more custodial care.

Since most of my patients are on Medicare, I saw many changes over the past two years. Trying to understand the whole dilemma, I tried to put issues in the right perspective. Yes, Medicare is draining the Federal budget and yes there should be changes and focus on the acuity of patients. But I realized most elderly people, who this program was designed for, are chronically ill with problems that won't go away, causing them difficulties with their activities of daily living. So the question is, where do we discharge these elderly patients to and what health care services can we arrange for them that don't cost much?

Each city and town has some availability to the elderly for home care services. There are "meals on wheels." That is a program set up to give at least one nourishing meal to the homebound and home health aides to help with custodial care on a sliding scale basis depending on the elder persons income; many cannot afford this, the patient is on a very limited income.

Agencies also have the worry of being charged with suspected "fraud and abuse." Fraud is defined as "intentional deception or misrepresentation that the individual makes, knowing it to be false, and that could result in some unauthorized benefit to them"

Some examples of fraudulence: billing for services or supplies not provided, altering claim forms to obtain a higher reimbursement amount or misrepresenting the services rendered, to name a few. Abuse is defined as "incidents or practices of providers, physicians or suppliers that are inconsistent with accepted sound medical practice.

This is unfortunate because statistics indicate that only three percent of all suspected fraud and abuse have any merit, the remaining 97% are misunderstandings.

I had an 80-year-old patient whom I had been seeing for the past year. She had hypertension (high blood pressure) and congestive heart failure and needed her blood pressure checked every 2-3 days. Frequently, her lungs would fill with fluid and I would have to call the doctor and get an increase in the diuretic she was on; or her blood pressure would drop because of dehydration. The problem was she needed to be monitored. But under Medicare rules if she stabilized, we needed to discharge her. The big picture was she'd stabilize for two or three weeks and then her lungs would fill up again; she was elderly, didn't understand the signs to look for, so after I discharged her she'd end up back in the hospital with congested heart failure. "What about relatives?" my supervisor asked.

"A niece in Minnesota, no one really, she'll end up in a nursing home," I said. Just what the patient didn't want; she wanted to maintain a level of independence and she wasn't really nursing home material.

And there were many of these cases. The old, the frail, the needy, looking you in the eyes as if to say "help me." And what's the message we are giving them? "Sorry honey, you're on your own, call your niece in Minnesota, rely on your neighbor when you have chest pain; these senior citizens are living in fear of what's going to happen next. We are keeping them alive through modern medicine, then deserting them.

What's the answer? Is there a solution to improving Medicare benefits and the controversial HMO's? Sure. Rebel! Call your legislatures, fight back, don't settle for no, fight for the services you want and need, and be sure, very sure of your rights. There is a patient's

Bill of Rights. Ask questions when buying into insurance plans. What doctors do they use? What hospitals do they affiliate with? And what's their mental health coverage? It is a citizen's inalienable right to speak up; a squeaky wheel gets oiled first. Make life as miserable as you can for the HMO's if you're not getting the proper health care. I find patients and their families have a hard time doing this. Why? Because there is only so much a person can deal with and when a patient is very sick, the family gets overwhelmed and the last thing on their agenda is to have to fight for their rights. I know, I was there and gave up. My husband and I couldn't deal with Dan's emotional state and face our insurance company full force. I wished I had had an advocate, someone who could have stood up for us, spoken in our behalf.

But what is sad is we shouldn't have to do all that! It's a waste of time and energy and it's wrong! My dad used to say to us growing up that something is right or wrong, black or white and where our health care system is heading is definitely wrong!

There are people out there helping, trying to change the system. There is an organization called "Physicians for a National Health Program" based in Chicago. Their goal is public awareness for a national health plan, as well as nurse's organizations, ad hoc committees to defend health care throughout the United States; and if you're a patient or family member not happy with the care your getting, you can call the department of public health or Medicare in your state. There are avenues to take, but it is the awareness of those avenues and the persistence it takes to follow through.

It is important to protect us and our loved ones from health care disasters and financial burdens. Remember, good health care and medicine is a public service and should not be treated as a business.

CHAPTER THIRTY-FOUR

Am I Burnt Out Yet?

Nursing was getting to me, big time. I was sick of illness, death, dealing with insurance companies and medical supply stores. Ordering supplies was becoming ridiculous! Finding the right supply company for the right insurance was a full time job. At times, I felt as if I wasn't taking care of the patient anymore. That was the easy part; the hard part was telephone calls, paperwork and the driving! Ugh! I was tired of putting 50 miles a day on my car and fighting traffic. Road Rage! No one being nice to each other, no manners or consideration for the other driver. I counted thirty cars going by me before someone let me out of the side street I was on, and that's because they were taking a right onto the street I was on. Yes, I was getting burnt out and I hated myself for it. My personality was changing. I was a grump, a grouch; my kids hated me! My husband told me to get a grip!

    I remember a story I had heard about ten years before about a nurse named Jen. She had been in nursing for over 25 years and evidently was at the end of her rope. She worked in a hospital, on a medical floor and had been taking care of a demanding patient all week. Jen was frazzled, at her wits end when the patient said, "Hey nurse, I need my water container filled." Jen flipped out. "Water container! Get off your lazy fucking ass and fill it yourself. What do you think I am your maid?" Jen left the patient's room, found the Nurse Manager and said, "I quit, I just can't take it anymore, I verbally abused a patient and I don't even care!"

I wasn't at that point yet; nor did I want to go there. What could I do to change things? I had to work for financial reasons, had two kids in college and one to go, I couldn't even cut down my hours! Worst of all I didn't want to start resenting my patients; they couldn't help it if they were sick, needed a nurse, I should be feeling bad for them when I show up at their door!

As I was contemplating feeling sorry for myself, the phone rang; it was a close friend, a friend from the past whose daughter was emotionally ill and brought me back to reality. Could I please meet her at the hospital? I pulled my frazzled self together remembering I was in this same position two years before with my son Dan, and headed north to the adolescent psychiatric unit at a New Hampshire hospital. My friend Mary Ann, whose daughter was 16, a sophomore in high school had overdosed on drugs; the school thought that it was intentional. Cynthia was sitting in English class, nodded out on her desk and couldn't be aroused. At the hospital, she had recovered physically but admitted she tried to kill herself. Mary Ann asked me to do private duty nursing for a couple of nights. The next two nights I baby sat, played "Sorry" and "Monopoly" with Cynthia and made sure she wasn't going to hurt herself again. When I went to the nurse's station about 5:00 to read Cindy's medical chart, a social worker named Alan, and a young 23-year-old female nurse were discussing Cindy's case. Jackie, the young nurse, said to Alan, "There are drugs at our high school? I can't believe it."

Alan, rolling his eyes, said, "Jackie, there are drugs in every high school in America!"

Jackie replied, "Not the high school I went to, no drug problems there."

Alan said, "So where'd you go "Doris Day" high school?"

I started to laugh with Alan. "Who's Doris Day?" Jackie replied. Alan said, "Doris Day was a movie star, in all of her movies her life was "peachy keen" and "hunky-dory." Jackie didn't get it, and looked at Alan with a dumb face.

I said, "Look Alan she'll find out soon enough life isn't "peachy keen" working in this joint."

Cynthia recovered, was amongst the normal in another week. Adolescents seem to have the ability to spring back to life as if nothing happened; one minute she's close to death, the next week she's doing cartwheels in her cheerleading uniform at a football game.

The next week I met Joan for lunch. Joan was the nurse who oriented me to visiting nursing over a year ago. I called her up and said, "Joanie, meet me for lunch. I need companionship and a good laugh." We met at Dunkin Donuts a few hours later.

With a big smile on her face, she put her arm around me and said, "What's the matter, Kate?"

"What's the definition of burnt out, Joan? Because I think it's happening to me."

"Been there," said Joan.

"What was your absolute worse day, Joanie, and did it get better?" I asked.

Joan told me how she was working as a nurse's aid while she went to nursing school. She was exhausted, never sleeping; work and school was her life. Except Fridays no matter what, Friday nights she went to a disco, danced all night long. "My mother hated me going, told me I should stay home, study, get ready for work the next day," she said.

Evidently, Joan partied hard one night arrived home at 3 a.m. and set the alarm for 6:15 a.m. to make it to work by 7 a.m. The alarm didn't go off on time; at 6:45, she jumped out of bed, grabbed her clothes, quickly dressed and pulled up to the parking lot of the nursing home. She jumped out of the car, looked down at herself and realized she was only wearing her bra, white panty hose and blue sweater, she forgot to put on her uniform!

She realized she was too exhausted to work, went home and called in sick! The rest of the day, driving to see patients I kept laughing, picturing Joan standing outside of her car, half naked, holding her uniform!

After meeting with Joan I became hopeful; maybe my career wasn't over; Joan had felt burnt out and recovered, so couldn't I! I would rally; become the good nurse once again.

CHAPTER THIRTY-FIVE

End of the Journey

My mom had gotten sick in June of 1998. She was 92-years-old, had never been sick a day in her life and doctors couldn't find a definitive diagnosis for her. "She's dwindling" my sister Denise's boyfriend, Alan said. Alan is an ER doctor and therefore qualified to know. How often I had heard the terms dwindling and dying. But I didn't want to apply it to my mother. The fact was she was dwindling; she had lost her spirit and her will to live. Her beautiful green eyes were fading. Getting closer to death every day, she was at the end of her journey.

The beginning of July she started dragging her left leg. Her doctor had her admitted to a rehabilitation center to try and have a physical therapist work with her. But she developed a blood clot in her leg and she went downhill from there. Her bowel perforated one night while Denise and I were visiting. She suddenly became cold, clammy, started to shiver then vomited up bile. The ambulance quickly transferred her to the Emergency Room at Laureat clinic; after a cat scan, she was diagnosed with cancer. A tumor was leaning on her bowel and caused it to perforate.

For forty-eight-hours I watched the nurses and aides take care of my mom. Rub her back, medicate her, turn and position her in bed, keep her pain free. I watched this beautiful Scottish woman who had brought me into this world slowly slip from it. Each of her seven children got to spend alone time with her before she died. I held her hand Sunday morning, heard her bracelet jingle, a familiar sound; it was a bracelet with charms of all her children on it, something she never removed. My mom turned looked at me and said, "Am I dying, Kate?"

I couldn't reply right away. Thirty seconds went by and I squeezed her hand and nodded yes. "Are you in any pain, Mama?" I asked, realizing I hadn't called her Mama in over 40 years. She shook her head "no" with a look of acceptance; she'd be with my dad soon.

My mom died about 4 am the next morning with my sister, Irene, at her side. She heard her take her last breath. Renie said she held her hand after she died and said the rosary and tried to absorb the fact our mother had just left this world. I had read somewhere that dying was as easy as walking from one room to another, the passage graceful and easy. My son, Chris, told me he felt his grandmother pass through his room at 4:30 am. And when the telephone rang at 5, he knew it was his Auntie Renie telling us Grammie had died.

Denise and I joined Irene in the hospital room and looked at my mother's blue tinged corpse. Denise said, "You've certainly seen better days, Mom." We laughed.

I said, "Well, Mary Connors, this is the first time I've ever seen you not striking up a conversation." My mother would have liked the humor.

It was her time, 92 years on this earth and never an illness. God had been good.

CHAPTER THIRTY-SIX

The Answer Is Yes

I had asked myself six months before if I was burned out of nursing. The answer turned out to be yes.

After my mom died, I went back to work the following week. My exhaustion continued as well as my apathetic state of mind. I thought maybe I needed a vacation. The last four years had been an emotional roller coaster and then with Mom's death I was having a hard time putting things in the right perspective. Maybe it wasn't nursing getting me down. I just hadn't taken care of "me" in so long that I probably needed to just get away.

In late October Gary and I went to visit his sister in San Diego. I relaxed, baked in the California sun and started to feel alive again. But a month after returning to work the burned-out feeling was returning. I was tired of the same old shit day after day, illness totally surrounding me. My territory at work had changed. I had to see more patients in a larger territory. "Oh, good," I said to my husband, "more road rage to observe!"

And I did. Two guys jumped out of their cars at a red light started beating each other up. A good reason to draw blood, he cut you off!

The world was insane, and I felt I was too, realizing our world was full of anger, rage, hate and depression. The world of Prozac, drugs to make you feel better, or was it drugs not to let you feel at all. "So sad. So sad," I mumbled to myself. Is there a cure for this universe? How do we fight the bureaucrats, politicians supporting a failing health care system, a system out of control? And our world so weary, where God doesn't matter, only money matters; it is everyone's God.

I realized as I headed to a patient's house that I was negative, losing perspective and losing hope in mankind. I was losing the belief that my generation could do something, anything to protect a health care system that was losing sight of the most important element, the patient.

I hated my negative attitude and wanted to be more positive. The next six months I made myself be happy. "Fake it till you make it," my son, Dan, said, "Take a happy pill. Remember when we were little and grouchy, you told us to take a happy pill."

I made a grateful list, everything in my life I was grateful for. And I was, to a point, sometimes saying how grateful I was through gritted teeth. My husband said, "Suck it up, Kate; lots of people don't like their jobs."

I tried to explain it was more than sucking it up. I need a career change."

"Like what?" my husband asked.

"I could open a coffee shop, sell books, read tarot cards have muffins and dessert."

"You'd have to bake, Kate," he said.

"Ugh," I replied, my family knew the best meal I made was cheese nachos about 10 at night! "I'll use my inheritance money to live on for a while," I said this with a hopeful look on my face, hoping my husband would say, 'Poor Katie, tired and burnt-out, go spend the only money we'll ever get in our life — our retirement money, I love you so much I want you to be happy. Spend the inheritance!'

Gary simply rolled his eyes, shrugged his shoulders and shook his head as he left the room.

I said, "You're getting sick of me whining aren't you."

"No," he said sarcastically.

"I feel like I'm at my job, listening to everyone complain all day; this is just a continuation, but the good part is I'm starting to go deaf so I'm only hearing bits and pieces; it's actually not bad, losing your hearing!" Ha! Ha!

I said, "You're a big help." At least I was guaranteed one thing, I could always find humor at home!

CHAPTER THIRTY-SEVEN

The Guiding Light

So where do I go from here? A question I had no answer for and decided to leave my fate up to destiny. Let a higher power, a guiding light direct me on to the path I should take. My daughter Jessie was graduating from college, and at the end of June we were going to meet my sister Irene in Seattle, spend a few days there and then drive the coast of Oregon and California, ending up at Renie's house for a few days. I would find answers about my fate along the way, pray on Trinidad Beach, hope God would enlighten me as to what I should do next.

I would be a nurse thirty years in September. Could I continue with this career for another twenty years until retirement? Certainly not with the way I was feeling. Before I left for vacation, I had three difficult weeks. A patient named Ethel Stenopolous was keeping me busy. Ethel was an 80-year-old widow, missed her husband who had been dead for three years, cried for him and occasionally felt he was still in the house. She was a diabetic needing daily, then twice a day insulin injections but was unable to administer the insulin injections because of her increased memory loss. A social worker was trying to convince her to go to an assisted living facility where she would be safe. Every morning I gave her insulin and a half hour later, she'd call the office looking for me, telling the secretary I hadn't been there. I would get paged, "Mrs. Stenopolous called and is waiting for you to give her insulin so she can go out," the secretary would say.

"I was there one half hour ago and she's not supposed to go out. I'll call her."

So, I'd call. "Ethel, I was there. I gave you your insulin."

"Oh, I forgot," she said.

"And don't go out. You're homebound." (Medicare rule).

I'd try to convince her to go to a nursing home.

"No, no nursing home. I'm not leaving this house."

There was no solution. She wasn't incompetent, could still make decisions; we could only hope for the best.

Two days later, I found Ethel walking up her street. I stopped the car and said, "Ethel, you're supposed to be home."

"Look, lady," she said angrily. "I'm going to Demoulas food shopping, then to the hair dressers."

I said, "Ethel, how are you getting there?"

"Walking," she replied.

"But its four miles from here and you're not supposed to leave your house."

She pulled her hair out on both sides and said, "Look! Look at this hair. Would you want to walk around looking like this?"

I started laughing and said, "You get back to your house now! It is raining and you're not walking anywhere."

She turned around and went home. I tried to explain, once again, she was unsafe leaving the house.

"But look at my hair," she said.

Joking around I said, "Look Ethel, you look great with an Afro!"

***

I went for a walk with my girlfriend, Lois, one evening and told her I needed a career change. Lois was a friend with whom I met through our town hockey program, our sons had played together for many years. She joked around and said, "Be a time keeper for hockey games or go to referee school. They always need refs!"

I pictured myself helmet on, the black and white striped shirt and pants, hockey skates, refereeing a bunch of out of control hockey players, getting sworn at and booed off the ice. "Not for me, Lois, but I would be a Zamboni driver." I was always mesmerized as the Zamboni cleaned the ice going slowly in circles, not missing a spot, no patches of ice unclean.

Work became increasingly busy after the summer ended. Labor Day had come and gone. I had many patients at one assisted living facility and would spend half my days there. It was a beautiful development with gorgeous landscaping and an area to sit on a sunny day in front of the building. The residents would line themselves up in chairs and watch as people parked their cars and entered the building.

I realized the elderly population says exactly what is on their minds, good or bad, they don't hold back. What do they have to lose?

Probably at this point in their lives they're not caring what people think, whose feelings their hurting!! I'd feel their eyes upon me as I got out of my car and locked the door. One man yelled out, "Nice legs."

"Thanks," I said.

A female resident said, "What you have on doesn't match!"

Two days after Labor Day being very hot and muggy, I wore a pair of shorts and a white blouse. A resident yelled at me as I was walking in the door, "Don't you know you're not supposed to wear white, ever, after Labor Day?"

One day while jogging around a local pond, an elderly man stopped me and said, "You've been running around this pond for at least ten years. Haven't you?"

"Yes, almost twenty," I said.

"Well," he continued, "I've been watching you and you've never lost any weight. Have ya?

I even remember my own mother on her deathbed telling my nephew he was much too fat! *What gives?* I thought. *I guess its elderly rights or something, criticize or compliment, get whatever is on their minds off of it.*

And so it went. I continued with my career. I moved on to a level of acceptance, for a while anyway. I was taking a day at a time, not looking too far ahead, trying to find what I had lost, the passion to be a nurse. I remembered a few months before, our plane ride to Seattle looking over at my 22-year-old daughter, a recent college graduate. She was wide-eyed and eager, full of enthusiasm for life, for her new job as a counselor. What could she do to hold on to her passion, not burn out from our sick health care system; a tired system where making money was the main goal?

I fervently hope that efforts are made and continue to be made to avoid the possibility of a defunct Medicare system and that there will be a change in consciousness in the United States regarding health care and health care workers. And that we are all brought together, cohesiveness, in participation in making this a better, a safer and more compassionate and caring world to live in.

Thirty years ago, I thought I was going to become an artist. Just as painters work with paint and create beauty, nurses learn the art of caring, the art that involves feeling, needs and experiences of people when they are under stress. Nurses are there when babies are born, old people die, human beings are ill or injured and it is up to us nurses, as a collective group, to keep this art of caring alive so that it can be passed on, generated into the next century so it won't end up a lost art, so that we will able to continue to enlighten the next generation.

EPILOGUE

August 1999

The traffic on route 128 heading south was backed up for miles. "Cape Cod Traffic," I said to my son Chris. We were heading to Canton, Massachusetts, about thirty miles from my house, so Chris could go to an off ice training school. Christopher is a hockey player, heading for Sweden the end of August with Team Massachusetts for fourteen-year-olds. All the driving and running around in preparation for the tournament would be worth it; Sweden at age fourteen.

I pulled my car into Blue Hills Regional High School an hour later. "Have fun," I said to my son. "I'll be back in a couple of hours."

"You're not going to stay and watch?" he asked.

"Not today buddy, there is something important I need to do," I replied.

Ten minutes later, I was in front of Canton Children's Hospital now called Massachusetts Hospital School, where my thoughts of being a nurse emerged over thirty years ago.

I parked my car, reached in the back and grabbed a blanket, notebook and pen; spread my blanket right next to the little bridge, the walkway that connected buildings. Not much had changed in all these years. Had thirty-two years really passed? It seemed like yesterday I was walking over the bridge, sixteen-years-old, a kid myself wheeling little Lisa in her wheelchair or holding my sister Denise's hand as she grasped the railing for support after being bed bound for nine months.

Tears came to my eyes. People in white uniforms passed by looking at me curiously, wondering why I was sitting on a blanket crying. *Happy tears,* I thought.

A gentleman in a green outfit crossed the bridge and glanced over at me. As he leaned over the side of the bridge, I could see he was a hospital employee, his nametag was on his attire. "Are you okay?" he asked.

"Sure," I replied, "just a little nostalgic. My sister had scoliosis and had surgery here, over thirty years ago."

"Just thought you'd come and visit?" he asked

"Of course," I said. "It's good to go down memory lane once in a while. I decided I wanted to become a nurse after my sister had surgery. This is where it all began for me".

"Tough profession," he said. "Nurses are not respected as they should be and they work so hard."

How true! I thought. And women are becoming aware of that. There has been continued decline in nursing school programs, baccalaureate level as well as hospital schools. Some are even closing; some of this is due to hospital downsizing and the knowledge of nursing lay offs, as well as the restructuring that is taking place throughout the health care industry. Furthermore, young women (I say women because over 90% of nurses are women) are finding jobs with less stress, more respect and higher salaries. Most professions are open to women now, compared to thirty years ago when most girls chose nursing, teaching or the humanitarian professions. New graduates from nursing programs are lucky if they start out at $30,000 per year with little potential of advancing quickly, where the computer industry or the business world may start out between $30-40,000-per year with the potential of making double that in a few years.

I reflected on all the people I had taken care of in the last three decades. In September, it would be thirty years since I embarked on my career. I had taken care of hundreds, even thousands, of patients. I had learned something from each one of them. Had I made a difference in their lives? Some I did. A few became friends.

I thought of the eagerness, passion and enthusiasm I had for nursing when I started out; the wide-eyed nursing student, eager for knowledge, wanting to help and heal. What happened? Probably a combination of things. The ever-changing health care system that enables us to burn out. Less staff, more work, insurance companies running the show, telling us when a patient should be discharged or no longer needs nursing services. Fifteen years ago a patient stayed in the hospital until they got well enough to be discharged; the way it should be. Instead they are going home with wide open infected wounds, intravenous antibiotics and even home I.V. chemotherapy, tubes with drainage emerging from different parts of the anatomy, family members having to take care of their loved one, learning to be nurses in 24 hours, no choice, without a second thought from our mismanaged (they call it managed care) insurance companies. Ignorance is bliss, "Wish I didn't know now what I didn't know then," the Bob Seger approach.

I took a personal look at my life in the last three decades and how far I'd come. It wasn't often I looked in the rearview mirror of my life but every once in a while it was important to do. Look back; learn from mistakes so you try not to make them again. Drug addiction. How sad my world had been then and what I learned from the experience. I was a lost soul who found her way back; amazing grace. Yes, it was important to peek, glance into the rear view mirror but not stare, it was over, the past, time to move on and I was grateful.

At quarter of six, I tossed the blanket in the back of the car and headed towards the school to pick Chris up. I didn't know where I was headed with my profession, even if I would stick with nursing, but I knew with time, the answers would come. What I did know was that it was my obligation to do something politically about changing the health care industry.

"Don't be a spectator your whole life."

My dad used to say, "The world is full of spectators … watching, observing, complaining, never fighting for change; our social responsibility is to be a "doer" make a stand when necessary." I wasn't going to stand on a table, hold up a sign saying "union" like in Norma Rae, but what I could do was set realistic goals and fight for my profession, fight for what was right in health care, be a patient advocate, get involved.

Chris was playing street hockey with his friends when I parked the car. Fourteen-year-olds. What would the health care system be like for them in 40 years? How could our government change the system so it will still exist in 50 years to get Medicare? What a sad, weary world.

"You're late, Mom," Chris said as he hopped in the car. "Where have you been?"

"Oh, just looking back on the last thirty years and trying to figure out what to do with the next thirty," I said.

"Did you figure anything out?" he asked.

"Only that our society needs to start thinking of one another's welfare and be a more respectful society," I said.

He shook his head in acknowledgment; too young, really to understand the depth of my feelings. I wanted to be an artist again on some level, the art of healing, get regenerated as a nurse; but I was leaving it up to destiny, for now anyways until I could cut through the dark clouds of my profession seek clarity in the health care profession.

I went back to Laureat Clinic one morning to do some research in the library. My old stomping grounds that I was indebted to. I learned so much, was able to care for so many wonderful people where they received the best care medically, exceeding the rest. As I was leaving the library, I walked by the Chapel. In the sixteen years I worked there, I never once entered the Chapel. I told patients about it, directed families to the areas, but never myself walked through the doors. That day I did. I knelt down on a pew, prayed to God for guidance and thanked him for all I had done, what I had accomplished.

I thought of my dad; it was his birthday. If he were alive, he would have been 95. He had been such an inspiration to me, showing me determination when I was struggling through school. What advice would you give me now, Dad? Quit nursing? Make a career change?

"Make the best of it," he'd say. "Stick with it. You're a nurse, a professional, be grateful."

I left the Chapel with a renewed sense of hope. I was being watched over and would be guided. The answers would come.

Bibliography

Boston Globe, Thursday, April 5, 1984, "Massachusetts Legislatures Tour Troubled State Hospitals".

Family Physicians and Managed Care: A View to the 90s. Healthcare Decision Counseling, 1996 Health Responsibility Systems, Inc.

"Medicare Made Simple", Denise Kraus, pp. 5, 7, 305, 306. http://www.mgh.harvard.edu/about/overview.htm

New York Teacher; March 10, 1999.

Time Life Books, the Year in Review, 1969, New York, NY, pg. 47.

www.ingramcontent.com/pod-product-compliance
Lightning Source LLC
Chambersburg PA
CBHW052047070526
44584CB00017B/2090